MY STORY

DATE DUE

BRODART, CO.   Cat. No. 23-221

FROM S TO M

MY STORY FROM MS TO MS

Multiple Sclerosis:

Hiding a monster?
Or a Monster Sleeping?

Mark Stewart

CONTENTS

Thanking you for your continued support of
my efforts and my first book.

Please continue to make a difference.

"Together there is nothing we can't do."

Author, Mark Stewart, is a happily married father
of three boys.
Born in Toronto, and raised in Brampton,
Ontario, Canada,
he shares his unique life story and struggles with his
readers and shows them the true side of life dealing with
disabilities, illness and the constant fight of the unknown
disease . . . **Multiple Sclerosis.**

This book is dedicated to:

my beautiful wife, Arlette, who has continuously
stayed by my side through thick and thin for the past
twenty-five years.

She stayed through the drama though she thought it
would be a comedy.

Thank you. I love you.

ACKNOWLEDGEMENTS

- My family, Arlette, Randy, Jason and Dylan. You guys are my inspiration and my reason to live

- My Father and best friend, Al. There in a heartbeat for anything and everything, My Mom, Steven (Stay thirsty my friends), Janice, Stephanie, and Christopher

- My Sister and Brother in-laws, Joanne, Rob, Amanda, and Stephen

- My Nieces, Shannon, Sherydan and Nephews, Matthew, Jamie, Nikki, and Tate

- My In-laws, Mary and Victor, always there even when so far away

- My extended family, Don and Sharon

- Johnny and Nancy Bower, who have become a major part of my life

- My friends, Patrick, Patrizia, Sandra, Nolan, Irene, Tammy, Barry, and Ariela, always having my back covered even if it is to kick it

- Trina Bell, for your caring and support

- Lenny and Sahar Whelan, for their support

- Sherry, for my life lessons, fine tuning my book and helping me find my inner peace

- All my PSWs (Personal Support Workers) who do so much for me

- Wikipedia, great for resource information

- A very special thank you to **OMS (Ontario Medical Supplies)** for believing and making this dream a reality.

- And all of you who read this and become a part of my life

- And don't forget M&M's

Each of you is an inspiration to me in one way or another and this book could not have been completed without you.

Thank you.

I want to add a very special thank you to a great friend and mentor in my life, Sherry Skibo, who has single-handedly taken this book to a whole new level with her wisdom and understanding of how my life is and has been with Multiple Sclerosis. She has given me a new lease on life and taught me how to find my inner peace and for this I'm forever grateful.
Thank you Sherry.

Preface

I have often, as a lot of people may have been able to do, put blinders on, put up a wall or just blanked things out, so to speak, in my life, some good, some bad, some happy, and some sad, but I think these are things that have defined me and made me into who I am today.

I will refrain from using the names of old friends or people who have been in my life so as not to infringe on the feelings or privacy of anyone who may prefer to remain anonymous.

I write this as a reflection and an insight into my life to try to understand, if I can, why I have **Multiple Sclerosis.** It is a chance for me to quietly contemplate and source out where, in my life, I may have triggered this disease causing it to raise its ugly head and, if so, what that may have been. Perhaps this book will cause others to reflect and ask themselves the same question, "What woke up the **M**onster **S**leeping?"

Let me emphasize that this may appear to be a horror story to some. This is definitely not our intended fairy tale life with the sweet happy ending we were so looking forward to. For us, coping with this disease has brought much misery to each of us in its own way and has caused much grief collectively and individually. It has become a frustratingly miserable existence for each of us on an almost daily basis and a painful experience for a great family.

It is my hope that people won't judge me or my family after reading this. I am simply and to the best of my recollection, writing of my own personal experience(s) in my life to date through an open heart. Putting my life's journey on paper so to speak, as seen through my eyes and remembered.

It is in no way meant to compromise anyone's feelings in any way. Everything that has occurred in my life, good, bad, or indifferent, has made me stronger and better prepared for my future. For this I say thank you.

This is a book for others who deal with illness, diseases or just need a break from the reality and stresses in their lives. I hope you enjoy my life story and come to understand why I am who I am and how I arrived at this point in my life. So sit down, grab a drink, put on the fire and let's get started. **Better make it a double.**

FOREWORD

What did I want from my life? What did I want my life to be? What the hell happened?

What did I want from my life?

I think I wanted to be a fighter pilot when I was young, but because of my fear of heights and claustrophobia (in addition to getting sick in a helmet at Mach 2), it seems those dreams would be grounded or put on hold permanently. I just wanted to be happy, healthy and have a great family. Well, as the song goes "two out of three ain't bad". I got the best family and that makes me super happy. Health became another issue.

What did I want my life to be?

I always thought my retirement, if I had one, would be a golden glorious time, full of happy memories with my wife, seeing our family grown with their own kids and having grandkids running around that would mimic what our kids were like as they were growing up. Unfortunately I do not see that at all now. I cannot see beyond the physical, mental and emotional pain of today. It seems I merely exist now from day to day, just wanting to get through it as best I can.

What the hell happened?

Multiple Sclerosis happened. I see the anger that **Multiple Sclerosis** has caused. I see and feel the raw pain and the sense of helplessness that the disability side of this disease has brought to our family. I'm sensing and experiencing the emotional erosion of a marriage because as my disability gets worse it is having an unhealthy impact on our happy outgoing life together. Sometimes it feels like we are slowly drifting apart, each surviving together yet apart. We love each other so very much but distance seems to rear its head more and more. I feel as if we are becoming more like a couple who have been married for fifty years in the fact that we are both exhausted from all that we have been through together already. We can no longer share those simple precious moments together as a couple and family that we used to take for granted. Going for walks, holding hands, holding each other, and sitting together on the couch while watching a movie. Playing with the kids, sharing their life experiences together and laughing with them. Holding each of them fully. My wife used to lay her head on my shoulder and just sleep. She can no longer do that. We can no longer cuddle as much as we want to and be affectionate with each other. The burden of responsibility is so heavy on my wife's shoulders. There is only exhaustion at the end of the day after her full day's work, then coming home to make dinner, take care of the kids, manage the household, and then there's me to care for. That is a lot for anyone to have to do.

I completely understand this but I feel that we need some us time too. Some time to wind down at night to relax, watch a movie or just stare into each other's eyes. Reconnecting again.

I feel so lonely in this body and in this life. I so miss and want the affection we once had and experienced in our life together, as a couple and as a family unit. I'm so anxiously seeking or trying to get it back. This disease can devastate a marriage, a family.

Side note: In this last paragraph is a very powerful statement. I said I see the emotional erosion of a marriage, when in fact I should say it is the incredible strength of a marriage through a brutal time. I want the outside to look in and say: "What strength they have!" and understand that this is what **MS** is. It is **More Strength** than ever imagined. I want people to see the real world of **Multiple Sclerosis**. It has been said why don`t I talk to a shrink and let him keep my thoughts and feelings in a file hidden away? I say why pay someone else to file it away when I can share it with the world for **free**. I can spread the word of **Multiple Sclerosis**. I can spread the word of the true struggles, the ups and downs and I can also share a message of hope, a message of how do we get through this together.

I see how much **Multiple Sclerosis** has hurt my family because I am not able to do things with them or for them that a normal person can do. I can't play in the park or on the street with the kids. I can't throw a ball or shoot a puck. I can't run . . . I can't jump . . . I can't swim . . . I can't skate . . . I can't walk . . . I can't drive them anywhere . . . I can't dance with my wife, I can't even stand beside her. I can't gather my family in my arms and just hug them all to pieces. I can't help with the household, I can't work. I'm typing this book with just the use of one finger. The list goes on and on. The anger of the debilitation of my disease and the affect it is having on them and in our family is evident in my kids' behaviour. The frustration and the outbursts are prevalent every day and especially in me. I can't do a lot of things like others but I know I can be a father like no other.

Side note: I must emphasize how much my family means to me and how blessed I am to have them in my life. I can't walk but I can talk. I can think, read and share stories or special moments with them. I thank God for them every day. They are my inner peace. I am so grateful for them.

I'm constantly wondering and worrying about winding up in a nursing home or long term care facility because of my safety and it is killing me inside. Seeing my family going to family functions without me is very hard to deal with or to even understand. I can just sit at home and wait for them to return. How do I stay positive or smile when my life is turned completely upside down?

Side note: I understand that they must get out and try to have a normal life as well, but I say, "Hey, don't forget about me." It's not their fault I'm sick. It's in my genes. I just hate being alone. I have asked, "Why can't we do our family things here at our house where I can be a part of it, instead of me sitting here crying all alone?" I don't want to sound selfish. I just want to try to be included in family events now more than ever.

I wonder if this desire of wanting to be included is something I can eventually block out or delete from my memory somehow. I'm trying but so far it is not working very well.

I did not ask for a disability, I did not go shopping for one, I was given one for whatever reason and I hate it. I hit myself with things and beat myself black and blue, literally and I beg for death constantly. This is the wrong thing to do, especially in front of the children, I know, but I just get past the point of no return with no hope in sight of anything changing for the better, only for the worse.

I ask, "Where is my miracle? Where is my chance to live out my dreams with **my** wife and **my** family?"

I have often thought of doing a Bucket List but I just don't set limitations or goals on my life or follow rules very well. But one goal I would have added to it if I had made a Bucket list, and if I had foreseen my future, would have been to write a book or story about my battles with **Multiple Sclerosis** and for it to be published before I died. This is something that has become very near and dear to me and a great way for me to vent my daily angers and frustrations. I've never even kept a trophy or award as I just don't want accolades of what I accomplished during my lifetime. I know what I have done. I don't need something to collect dust to remind me. I guess my Bucket List would have probably just started with an <u>F</u> instead of a <u>B</u>. Life has changed my outlook now so instead of an <u>F</u>' it List I would have a Pray To Do It List as opposed to a Bucket list. But let's see how it goes.

A very special award that really touched me though was from my city for being the Inspirational Citizen of the Year. I know that I have made a difference somehow and somewhere. I just hope it helped someone else consider making a difference too.

One thing that I have asked and do want from my life is that when I do die I be cremated and kept at home with my wife and to be placed with her for eternity. (Jokingly . . . I want my urn to have googly eyes and a plaque that says I'm not an ashtray because I want to be kept beside my wife on her end table.)

This is my life in a nut shell. Let's delve into it a bit more and see if we can discover what may have been a reason for this disease raging inside of me today. Let's see if we can find out what happened and what may have awakened the proverbial **Monster Sleeping**.

DISCLAIMER

The views expressed in this book are mine and mine alone and do not reflect or promote any products or services or medications in anyway. The following is the author Mark Stewart's personal opinion and life, and is not the opinion or policy of the little M&M's people that have been following him all day. I, the author of the content that can be found here within, can assure you, the reader, that any of the opinions expressed here are my own and are a result of the way in which my highly disorganized and somewhat dysfunctional mind interprets a particular situation and or concept.

Enjoy . . .

In The Beginning

I cannot really recollect early memories of my life before the age of five it seems. (So technically at the time of this writing, in my mind I'm thirty-six). I was born on a cold February day in 1969 (I say cold because every day is cold in February) as the rest of the world was dealing with the Vietnam War and brand new space exploration, most notably on July 20, 1969 when Neil Armstrong walked on the moon and takes his historic first steps at 02:56 UTC, uttering the most famous words in history: "That's one small step for man and one giant leap for mankind." This was, in fact, the largest television audience for a live broadcast at that time. The famous 747 made its maiden flight, and let's not forget Woodstock and the fast cars of 1969.

And then there was me entering this world that year. I was born in Toronto, Ontario, Canada at North York General hospital. I was told my Mom had worked as a nurse prior to me being born and my birth father was a career mechanic. My parents had two children, myself and my sister Janice, who was born in September, 1971. Because, as I mentioned, I have no memory of my early years before the age of five or so, the following becomes sort of historical information.

My parents divorced when I was three or four years of age, so this may have been the traumatic incident which doctors would talk about later in my future that may have had a profound effect on my life. It quite possibly may have been a defining factor in forming my personality and a driving force throughout my life in my growing years after that. This became the first of many trials and tribulations that would enter my life and may have been what started to awaken the **M**onster **S**leeping.

I never asked why my parents divorced as I had no interest to do so. It happened and seemingly we all moved on in one way or another. I have a relationship with my biological father now as good friends and we're both happy about that. When my Father asked me to give us each a chance I was agreeable to it and our current relationship grew from that. I don't ever remember meeting my biological grandparents on my birth father's side or hearing anything about them. Not even sure if I'm anything like them.

It seems my first claim to fame was when I was two years old as I got to name my sister. I was told by my Mother all I would say was "Nanice, Nanice" so I'm not sure what I was talking about (I was probably saying "No Leafs, no Leafs"). But, as a result of this the name of my new sister became "Janice" Rae. Not sure where Rae came from but it seems to suit her. She even had a truck named after her later on in her life. (I will explain soon.)

So there we were, two kids against the world and what a world it was set to be.

My sister had her dolls and other girl toys and I'm sure I had my own toys which I'm certain had something to do with hockey. I do remember my sister telling me about her earliest memory of a doll called Mrs. Beasley that she had when she was around the age of two. How she could remember anything at this age is amazing to me as I cannot remember anything before the age of five. She said she remembers she got into trouble for whatever reason because she was in front of the television or something like that, and this was when she was only two (what a memory). I don't remember getting into trouble for anything. Maybe I was just a good kid? (**Not likely!**)

I remember my Mom telling me I would sniff things and say, "Fishy fishy." What this meant I have no idea. I may have blocked this and other things from my memory or just don't remember it at all. I can still block things from my mind and do so to the present day when things really annoy me. (It is like a light switch in my head.)

I would say something rude, arrogant, disruptive or disrespectful and then forget it within ten minute. Like: **clap-on, clap-off.** I will be more clear later I'm sure, or maybe I won't. Oops: **clap-off**.

Later on in my life my Doctor would ask me a strange question and it would trigger something in my mind. This would make me start to really wonder about things in my life and this is why I thought of writing this book.

The Doctor would ask me, **"Did you have a traumatic incident as a child or something that may have triggered this?"**

It makes me think now, could this have been it? Was it something I was blocking out or would there be something else that will come up later in my future?

My earliest memory is when I was possibly five or six, a couple of years after my parents had divorced. I truly can't remember anything at all before this. I was always playing with my cars (Hot Wheels) or watching hockey on television. I remember playing hockey in a hallway or room and playing with my cars, crushing the crappy ones and building a makeshift junkyard so I could destroy the ones I didn't like and store them there. Again I don't have the memories of ages two to four for some reason or maybe I've blocked them out. I'm just not sure.

My Grandmother (R.I.P.) used to tell me I would shoot pucks at her bedroom door all day long, driving her absolutely nuts and this was before I could even walk properly. So I guess my love for hockey started at or before the age of one. My Mother recently said there was always some sort of hockey equipment, a ball or a puck on me or with me or being shot around the house nonstop. I recently saw a picture of me with big hockey gloves on and a little hockey stick. The gloves were almost as big as me.

I remember my Mom telling me about my first day of school with my little yellow raincoat (I saw it in a picture). I remember her telling me that I had said, "Well, I'm glad that's over with. What now?" I thought that I only had to go to school once and then it was finished. Boy, was I wrong. (It's so funny that I said that as all three of my boys have said the same thing.)

I believe my Mom met my Father when I was about five. My earliest memory of this era is when we lived on Jane Street in Toronto, I remember vaguely the building we lived in and the halls and the general layout of our apartment.

I'm told often that when I was very young I would get into everything. (So much for "fishy fishy".) Well, apparently when we lived in the apartment there was a day that I allegedly (it was never proven in a court of law) started to throw my Dad's tools over the balcony and people started to gather in the street as they were now getting free tools. They were all yelling so I was getting excited and began throwing more and more for them to collect. We lived on a lower floor so there were a lot of tools landing on the overhang as well as on the grass below. See I'm always giving to other people, even back when I was only five. My Dad said there were hundreds and possibly thousands of dollars worth of tools that went over that balcony. He definitely was not happy. I still to this day hate tools and fixing things. So maybe that's the reason I can't fix anything, but I can certainly break things that's for sure. I have also built upside down cabinets and a Barbeque that could open both ways. Who said you don't need power tools to build a BBQ?

I always remember loving hockey. I don't ever remember liking a specific team until I was about ten years old. My Mom even had a picture taken of me wearing a Leaf shirt. (What was she thinking?) I remember Saturday Night Hockey games and soaking up the great knowledge of "hockey".

The New York Islanders and the Pittsburgh Penguins were it for me. I remember I loved Billy Smith (I actually met him later in my life). I admire him greatly, still do. And Mike Bossy along with Brian Trottier (both whom I've met as well) and I loved the Penguins Goalie, Michel Dion. He had the coolest mask. It looked sort of like a duck's bill. I have been a diehard Penguins fan for over thirty years now. I always loved to play goalie and when my cousins and I got together when I was very young, I was always the goalie for every game. I loved Billy Smith and would pretend I was him and even painted a set of my pads to be like his.

I was never a Toronto Maple Leafs fan, even though my Mom got that horrid picture taken but this would change later in my life to some degree. Let's jump back to when I was ten or so. My Dad was a big Toronto Maple Leafs fan so it was easy.

It was like a competition for me to like another team it seemed. I remember Dad and I would bet quarters on games between Pittsburgh and Toronto (how do you think I paid for my house?). I would never follow anyone even when it came to which hockey teams I liked.

My Dad liked the Leafs and I liked the Penguins and this has become a life's obsession.

Side note: Isn't it funny that no other sports team is named after something that isn't even a word? Leafs? Shouldn't it be Leaves? What's a 'Leafs'?)

I was able to make one of my Dads dreams come true later in life as well. My Dad, Alexander Stewart or Stu to all his friends was always a super hard working, there for everybody, kind of person and still is to this day. He has driven a truck throughout my entire life (hence my love for trucks as well). This is why my sister's name was on his truck (*because she is spoiled*). I remember the big white truck with the big red display board saying "**JANICE RAE**." I believe he changed to an orange truck shortly thereafter.

I still think it should have been called "**MARK's Rig**". I will tell you more about my Dad's dream later on.

My parents were and have been foster parents from the time I was very young. I can remember that we always had different kids living with us. Throughout my life we were always with another child or children who needed my parents help. It was wonderful to have so many kids in our family. It felt kind of like we got a new brother or sister every month or so. Sometimes I wish we could have sent my sister away or trade her in for a hockey stick. I have wondered if fostering these children took away from any attention that we may have needed or that I may have been craving from my parents. It never ever seemed we were neglected by my parents because I'm positive that never happened. I was always very proud of my parents and all the work they did to help others which later in my life would eventually become a major part of my life. I think I owe it to them for giving me my passion for helping others. I think to this day they have watched or help raise over one hundred and fifty kids and my Mom is still going strong watching little ones.

I remember going to a public school in Toronto where I lived. I grew up at Jane and Finch, a very rough, tough neighbourhood in Toronto even back then and it seemed I struggled with it. I remember kids not wanting to share with me or stealing my marbles or hockey cards. (I know, I lost my marbles at a young age.) I have a vivid memory of fighting with a boy in the playground because he said I was not good enough for the slide. I think I was seven. I had to fight for my place many, many times throughout my life and developed quite a shield, temper and attitude because of it. I think I made my point in the playground because I played there quite a bit after that. I never even told my Mom about this encounter at that time as I guess I thought I was supposed to be the man of the house so to speak and the big brother. I actually forgot about this incident until I was writing this chapter and it came flooding back to me.

I also remember the big hill at my school and sliding down it in the winter during recess and every other chance we got. It seemed like the biggest hill in the world but I was only five or six so what did I know. Ah, good times! But I learned to keep a lot of the problems I was having or issues inside for many, many years. It would all explode eventually.

I remember the hallways in my building where I grew up were rough and the older kids would be hanging around in the stairwells. We would only use one set of stairs in that building because we didn't want to run into the big kids.

I remember collecting pop bottles from people in the building so we could get candy money. We spent a lot of time playing hide and seek and playing hockey in the underground garage. And then there is my infamous running into the elevator just as the doors closed and crushed my head. We were playing cops and robbers in the hallways and I was the cop (wow, there's a change). I was chasing my friends as they ran into the elevator because 'they were trying to escape'. They were pushing the button repeatedly and attempting to close the elevator door as I was running towards it full speed yelling, "Freeze! You're under arrest!" Well, the doors started to close so I made my move and I dove head first into the elevator, but the doors had closed too far and I got my head stuck in the door opening between both doors. My head split wide open (so much for my Olympic diving career). This was probably my first concussion and I never even knew it at the time. A young soft head involved in a traumatic incident like this may have started the ball rolling in my future.

I remember going down the stairwell bleeding all over the rails, trying to get home to show my Mom. Off to the hospital for more stitches.

So I guess my first run in of many physical incidents, and emotional ones, was when I was only seven years old. It wouldn't stop there.

I also remember a lot of good times as well. Playing ice hockey and winning championships, listening to "WE ARE THE CHAMPIONS" by Queen and saying "Yeah this is cool!" I would get to hear that song many more times in my life in different sports, but alas, never on a professional level. I thought I was going to be a super star hockey player (goalie) in the NHL, but I ended up becoming just a super fan and lover of my favourite sport, Hockey. It continues to this day over forty years later, but more on hockey further on.

It seemed I always got what I wanted or needed. I remember being quite spoiled and having the coolest toys, along with tons of hockey cards and hot wheels. I used to play hockey cards with my friends in the hallway and remember being quite good at it. I used to put hockey cards in my bike tires and make it sound like a motorcycle. (Yep, I was a rebel.)

I remember one time my Dad got an over shipment of Hot Wheels on his truck and that meant they came home with him. I had thousands and I mean thousands of these things. They were stacked all over my bedroom from one end to the other. They were boxes of 12 cars to a box and I think there were about 500 boxes. I loved them all. I had cities made for all my cars, a special place for the cool ones, and a junkyard for the old ones that I replaced. I spent hours playing with my cars. I recall having over-shipments of gumballs, chocolates and Turtles (the chocolates). I still don't like them much to this day.

I've always loved the outdoors and my bikes. I say bikes because I broke so many and then I would come home with them in separate pieces and say "Grandpa, I broke another one." He would fix me and the bike up and have me riding the trails the very next day. My Grandfather (R.I.P) was a tough, very strong man but at the same time as gentle as a giant teddy bear (I have a funny story of him later in the book as well). I used to ride across the street from my building on the large trails where the big kids used to ride motorcycles. Not for kids but that didn't stop me. I rode my bike on every trail and jumped every jump. I had no fear it seemed.

I remember riding down a long trail that ended with a big downhill and then a huge jump. I recall flying through the air and seeing that a guy on a motorcycle was coming out from underneath me and thinking, "Oh boy! This is going to hurt!", and **BANG**—I landed right on top of him. "I broke another one, Grandpa." I broke my bike into three sections and there was no repairing this one. I got my next new bike and was so very proud of it. I even let a so-called friend ride my new bike. He never came back with it. "Grandpa, I need another one." I think in my life I have gone through thirty bikes. I have crashed twenty of them for sure.

I use to play cops and robbers as I had mentioned and I would go overboard to make a dramatic death scene when it was my turn to get shot. I once was standing on a bridge at two major intersections (Jane and Steeles) and my friend shot me with our potato gun (it would shoot small pieces of potatoes. I'm not even sure where we got the potatoes from) so to make my death look cool I leaned over the bridge, too far I'm afraid, and down I went, right into Pioneer Village and the creek below (about twenty-five feet), but at that age the fall seemed to last forever. It was full of rocks and not much water. I cut myself up pretty bad and remember a lady in a car stopped and came running down the hill beside the creek, climbed over the fence and bent over me. She gave me her shirt to try to stop the bleeding (very exciting moment as I got to see my first bra). She then drove me home to my Mom where I was promptly marched off to the hospital. I ended up with stitches in my head and foot but they would certainly not be my last. And remember the elevator incident? Yeah, that had cost me a hospital visit and stitches too.

I was recently talking to my parents about this and they have their version of what happened in the hospital. I say I was cool, calm and collected, but my parents say I was a crying lunatic. I guess parents are always right. I don't remember but it is what they tell me and everybody else about this incident.

I try to look back at what I may have been hiding from or what may have been haunting me, so to speak, all my life to make me who I am today and wonder if this was the beginning of all hell breaking loose and quite possibly the onslaught of what would became the future of me with **Multiple Sclerosis.**

Reflecting back I remember being about nine when my Mom came to me and asked about changing my last name to Stewart. She had been dating my future Dad, Alex, for a while and he was the greatest thing since sliced bread to me. I was so excited to take on a new identity so to speak. I remember proudly telling my friends at school I was getting a cool new name, Mark Stewart. This is who I was and who I would become.

Just a flashback I think I was six. We had moved around a bit and I remember living in Calgary for a while in a white and blue house with a big window in the front, so my Mom could always see whatever I was doing. I remember riding my bike and making jumps like Evel Knievel (my then hero). I remember a jump that didn't end well as I crashed right into a pickup truck while I was in the air. Why he parked there I'll never know. I landed in the back of his truck. I also remember my best friend, Mark Flood (I would later in life hear that he committed suicide at a very young age). But that is really all I remember about Calgary. We returned to Toronto again and my life got kick started once more. I thought I would forget about that part forever.

I remember snow ball fights and throwing snow at the cars that passed by on Jane Street. Then we would hide behind a giant sign at our building on the corner of Jane and Finch but all in all that was a place I was glad to leave. (Throwing snow balls at cars would get me in big trouble later in life as well.) I remember a time when we were at my cousin's house and we decided to go to the corner store. We were throwing snow balls at each other and I decided to throw one at a car coming down the street. I stood out in the middle of the street, threw the snow ball and wham, right off his windshield it flew. I immediately ducked behind a car. All I heard was the skidding of a car's tires and then some guys yelling "Get him!!" That was my signal and in a flash I was gone. I ran into the store and jumped right into a potato chip rack so I could hide. My cousin was still standing outside with no idea what had happened. He saw me run and I'm sure he thought, "Oh great! Now what did Mark do?" But he would not get a chance to ask that question as the guys began to chase him. He ran for blocks and blocks and when I saw them gone I raced back to my Aunt's house, quickly sat down and watched television, too frightened to tell her what happened. After a while my Aunt asked where my cousin was. I said he saw some of his friends and went off with them. I guess about thirty minutes had gone by when my cousin came into the house and yelled, "Where the hell is Mark?" Well, the guys from the car had gotten hold of my cousin and beaten him badly. So the men in our family went out to find the guys that beat up my cousin. Meanwhile I made myself a sandwich, but I did get in huge trouble later over this. No more snow balls for me after that (for a while anyway).

I had tons of fun back in those days with my cousin. Going to High Park, the mall and playing street hockey on the street and in the school behind his house. I remember going to the very first monster truck show with him as they lived very close to Exhibition stadium in Toronto. I would later visit this stadium for concerts and sports events more times than most people can imagine. I've seen hundred of concerts and many monster truck shows. I even got the chance to ride in one in Saskatchewan after winning a ticket raffle at a monster truck show but that was later in life.

I remember we had a very nice trailer that we would go to in the summers, to get away from all the hustle and bustle of life I guess, but when you're nine years old a trailer is a cool camping get-away for a kid. I would ride my bike around the park with hockey cards in the spokes like my bike was a motorcycle and I was king of the world. Everybody there knew me. They would say hi as I rode by on my way to the jumps my friends and I made in the overflow area. I was always doing something crazy while playing with my friends. We had a general store that we would hang out at to play pinball or even take dares from the older kids. I once ate a grasshopper for a KISCO ice treat. I think they only cost 10 cents, but I loved them (KISCO's, not grasshoppers). The kids would dare me to jump my bike or do some other crazy stunt and I would always be happy to be the crazy one. I remember falling out of a tree and through a barn roof onto the hay bales set up inside for a dance later that night. Yep, there was a nice hole in the roof for the night of the dance, but no one found out it was me. I remember one time playing bike tag and jumping out of the bushes when my cousin was coming and yelling "**GOT CHA!**" Well, he collided with me and his bike skidded right across my chest. Off to the hospital, again, for X-rays. Speaking of the hospital, once, while at the trailer park, I challenged my Mom to a fight (I used to think I was a great boxer). We were fooling around and she yelled, "**HEEEE YAAA**" and threw the greatest karate chop in history. Off to hospital again—broken collarbone this time. She was obviously a better fighter than me. She told me, "Please don't say it was me that hit you." Yep, you guessed it. I did. I said, "My Mother karate chopped me." I'm surprised they didn't say something, but it was an accident. I think!!

I remember the Collingwood trips we took and when I crashed on the great slide ride, scrapping my side really bad. This was a huge concrete slide approximately a thousand feet long that you would use a special sled on. I also remember how we annihilated the go-carts.

We kids at the trailer park even had a gang called the 'Warriors'. We made a fort in the woods and we would just hang around being cool (or at least so we thought). That's where I smoked my first cigarette (the start of one bad habit after another). We would ride our bikes through a farmer's corn field, destroying it, to go down to the Pine River which was a long ride when you're nine or ten years old. It was like an adventure. We would ride the trails and create more adventures as we went on our way. We always made sure we would be back before anyone knew we were missing. I was loving life. We had campfires at night and tons of activities to do during the day. All was good. I try to remember the good and the bad times and even the times that hurt, so I can look back and reflect where things may have gone wrong. I was a strong, determined kid who when you said "No Mark", I, Mark, would say "Why not!" and do it anyway, not thinking of the consequences or what effect it would have on me later in life.

I met my first girlfriend who was from Windsor and a cousin of a friend of mine at the trailer. I thought I was the happiest and luckiest kid then and nothing could ever go wrong for me. (Boy, was I to be mistaken.) Around this time in my life my body began rebelling big time and my family and I never had an inkling of what was yet to come. I had so much energy that you would swear I had Hyperactive Sensitivity Disorder. I was wired 24/7 and as a result my Mom had to put me on a special diet with no sugars at all. I had special breads, jams, peanut butter and absolutely no sweets of any kind. It was brutal and I remember fighting my Mom tooth and nail to have a snack. I think this situation lasted for less than a year. It was horrible. I mostly remember the taste of the peanut butter which to me was disgusting.

I also would work at the local Golf Putt Putt collecting golf balls when the driving range was closed. I think we got a dollar a bucket. I bought ice cream and other junk with my money. Money would burn a hole in my pocket. I was never a good saver. I would get a dollar and spend it before I could even remember getting it. I'm still kind of the same way.

I remember my friends and me riding our bikes to Shelburne from where our trailer was. I think it took us about two hours to get there. We would ride around for a while and then ride back to the trailer park. I even attempted to ride from Brampton to the trailer park one time for fun but didn't make it. I guess I was about eleven or twelve when being at the trailer became boring to me and I found myself not wanting to go back anymore.

A New Start

We moved from Toronto to Brampton in 1980 when I was ten or eleven and this is where most of my memories began. A new family member was born around this time as well. My brother was born in March of 1979. Although he is ten years younger than me he was to become a major role model for me and a great support in my future experience with **Multiple Sclerosis** I remember this little ball of fire filled with more energy than the sun itself. He would run around in circles and we would say he was going to go to China if he didn't stop. He was so funny. He has turned out to be a great guy with a great heart and I'm proud to call him my brother. I love you bro. (I will talk more about him later as well.)

I remember being the new kid on the street and meeting new friends right away. I went to a new school where I started grade six, was settling in fine, and met many more people.

Again I became very popular and made a lot of friends, some good, some not so good, and some just trying to find a way to fit in themselves. I remember 'shagging' the bus in the winter (being pulled behind the bus while holding onto the bumper) so we didn't have to walk to school (what was I thinking?). We would hang on for what seemed forever, then we'd eventually fall off and end up having to walk the rest of the way to school.

I had somewhere at this point requested to legally change my name to Mark Stewart. We had spoken of it in the past and now it was time. So now I had a new identity, but the same life that I was born into. My middle name, Bradley, came later and my Mom told me it was the closest name to 'brat' she could get. This will be news to a lot of people. (I'm just misunderstood.)

I remember playing school sports and excelling in whatever I did so, for me, I thought life was grand. I again remember having fights with people over territory and where we should hang out. The grade seven kids would try to start conflicts with me and I would not back down. I remember a girl told me I was so ugly she wanted to vomit and how hearing that really hurt me inside. My wall was raised once again and I put up another defensive shield in an effort to block out the pain. I guess we should always be careful of what we do and say to others and how we act as who knows what our futures hold and how someone's words can come back to haunt us, biting us in the butts when we least expect it. I wonder if I ever insulted anyone like this and they are saying, look at him now. I don't think I ever did. No, on second thought I'm sure I never did.

I had many fights between grade six and eight at that school. I remember teachers yelling at me and me saying, "Shut up already. You're boring me." A teacher even slammed me against the lockers because I stormed out of his class and broke the door's glass window when I slammed it shut on him. So maybe this is where it all began escalating. "All this anger" . . . I have never thought of these things again until now. I just keep burying everything deep in the darkest caverns of my mind.

I would always play foot hockey at recess or lunch time with friends in the school tennis courts. Sticks weren't allowed at school. (Good thing because I would have probably ended up accidently killing someone.) I remember the first signs of the unknown **MS Monster** back this far. I recall my legs shaking violently while I was sitting still. The teachers would even tie me to my chair because I was so fidgety. I fell over one time and I was left on my side for the entire class to 'teach me a lesson'. My legs would bounce up and down for hours. Everyone thought it was the extra energy I had because God knows I had energy to burn. I often have said that if I could have harnessed that energy I could have made a fortune. My body would jolt when I was relaxed and be completely violent when I was stressed. I would also tap my fingers on everything. It was totally insane.

I remember all the kids in my neighbourhood used to hang out at my house daily and even call my Mom "Mom". I remember the great hockey games we used to have and the hours we would put into playing our games, sometimes finishing at one or two o'clock in the morning. We would shovel the driveway for shooting practice and shovel the road for our games and even make boards. It was an everyday thing in the winter and a regular event in the summer as well. I also played ice hockey for my school teams and loved playing every chance I was given.

I also remember the gravel pits beside my house. They had a huge water hole in them and we used to go swimming in them regularly. We had to wait until the workers were gone as it was illegal to go in and the entire place was surrounded by a fifteen or twenty foot fence. We would climb it with no problems and play on the huge sand hills, then go swimming and just do whatever we wanted. I would go almost every day in the summer and on weekends as there were never any workers there during that time so we would be able to spend all day swimming, jumping in the sand hill and we even managed to get our bikes into the gravel pits. We were happy.

I remember one day we were hanging out there once around a six o'clock in the evening on a weekday. We were confronted by a fellow in a pickup truck who popped out of nowhere and surprised us big time. We went running up the hill as fast as we could to get out of the pit before we got caught. I recall he had some kind of gun thing because he shot at me with what seemed like salt. It hit my right leg, stung me so bad and left quite a mark. Painful! The next time we went we were very cautious of this happening again so we kept a watchful eye. Needless to say we went many times and truly spent wonderful hours there just having out and out fun.

We eventually found another gravel pit that was even bigger and better and we actually were allowed to ride our dirt bikes in it. We would pay a small fee to the workers to let us go crazy and burn off our extra energy and aggressions. This one had a huge water pit with two juts sticking out and we would jump off them into the water below. The cliffs were called the 'Tit Cliffs' because they looked like boobs from across the water. This location lasted for some time until one of our friends jumped and landed on a shopping cart that someone had thrown into the water. We were then ousted from this latest gravel pit and found ourselves looking for another one. Well, needless to say, we found one again, which was close to our house and we started to go there. It was five times the size of the others we had frequented and it had a huge cliff for us to jump off into the water, plus there were many sand hills. It even had telephone wires that crossed over the water which we would use as a spring board so to speak as they would fire us up in the air and into the water. This place was a hang out for a year or so for us until we eventually grew out of it.

It is strange to think about it now, just how dangerous it really was and how we could have been killed dozens of times. Jumps of fifty to sixty feet into water when we truly never knew what lay beneath the surface. Scary thought!

I remember having an ailment called Osgood Schlatters disease which is a very common cause of knee pain in children and young athletes usually between the ages of ten and fifteen. It occurs due to a period of rapid growth, combined with a high level of sporting activity. I remember having this when I was about eleven and having the full cast on my leg for months. I think this is where I was introduced to my first taste of real internal pain and it was unfortunately not the end of it by any means. I actually broke my cast off so I could play hockey. Unbelievable when I think of it now.

Grade seven is where the rebellion started. (People say it was long before this but I think it was here. At least this is when I actually became aware of it.)

I started smoking and being totally defiant. I had some strange eclectic friends and I was heavy into rock music. (I once bet my Mom that I would still listen to rock music when I was forty. We signed a contract and the bet was for One Hundred Dollars. I wish I had charged interest on that bet. Yep, she paid up). I grew my hair long, wore leather jackets and black clothes and was just in a very dark stage. I listened to a rock and roll band called Motley Crue and thought they were gods. My whole room was covered in posters of them. Needless to say my grades fell like the stock exchange and I failed grade seven. I thought, "Holy crap, another year of this hell." And yes, it was. I was sent to the office so many times that year I asked if I could carve my name on the desk. I remember doing projects on music and getting excellent grades as it was something I was interested in. Music and drawing and of course, sports. Maybe I had ADD (Attention Deficit disorder) that would have explained a lot. I failed again but they put me through to grade eight.

From the time I was very young I had an uncanny ability to draw what was imprinted in my mind. Almost like a photographic memory. I would see something and I could draw it with no problems, even long after seeing it.

I remember trading artwork for school work. I sucked at history so I would get the 'browners' to do my homework and in return I would do their art projects. I had found something I was good at.

I drew pictures of everything that was invading my mind, some dark, some evil and some with such beauty it was incredible, but I always remember ripping them up and saying they were not good enough. A pattern was growing. I did this still for many years and always wondered why. I also drew a school mascot that is still up to this day. It makes me wonder—HMMMMMM.

I had my first real girlfriend in grade seven. I thought I had found the meaning of life, not like my trailer park girlfriend when I was ten or eleven. We had what some would call a rocky relationship. It was constantly on again and off again like a light switch. We would either be very close and getting along great or we would be miles apart. But at fourteen who would know what was meant to be. I remember living with her family for a while as my parents couldn't handle me. I also remember spending a Christmas with them and the great duck we had for Christmas dinner. The duck was totally new to me as my exotic meal was grilled cheese with ham in it. Anyway, I believe we dated for about two and a half years.

I got my first tattoo while we were dating and she was not at all impressed. I had another one done and was going to put her name in it but my tattoo artist said, "No way Mark. You will never settle down and I'm not putting a girl's name on your arm. Come back to see me in ten years after marriage and thank me." Thank you. You were right. That could have been real awkward a number of times (more on the tattoos in the next chapter).

I remember their family's cottage and our getting away from the real world so to speak. It seemed like it was my get away from everything that drove me completely crazy. I truly admired her parents and sister. They were so kind to me. We would ride their dirt bikes and the dirt cars and just go everywhere. It didn't last too long though as we broke up again. I remember working with her Dad at a refinishing company. This was my first real job and I loved it. I still had a problem with authority but I kept all my problems stored away. I seemed to do quite well there and I never spoke up when things bugged me. I loved my job and tried very hard to learn the trade.

More jobs would follow later.

I developed this strange attitude like kids seem to do as they are maturing but mine was severe. I was very moody and aggressive. I would fight, yell, scream at my parents and totally disrespect anything I was told. I hated everything. School, kids, teachers, authority and was even told I was manic depressive because of my mood swings. I recall having an argument with my Mom. She raised her hand to me and I said "I DARE YOU." I had so much rage inside me and I didn't know why. I would never hit my Mom but I was just so angry inside.

One time I was at a store with a friend and he stole a cassette. We got caught and he begged me to take the blame as he was on probation and he would go to juvenile hall for sure. I told him, "Cool, no problem." And I took the fall. The police were called and came to the store. We were arrested and kept in a small room. I guessed it was meant to scare us but I thought, "What bullshit this is. Let's get it over with so we can catch the bus home." I remember the police coming in with their big tough guy attitudes and saying we were going to prison. They put us in the cop car and I, with my attitude, knocked on the back window and said "HOME, JAMES" like the cop was my chauffeur. That was not cool. He lost it and dragged me out of the car at the police station and nearly beat the hell out of me. I remember him putting a phone book on my head. I thought he was going to make me balance it. Then bang, he hit it and down I went. I guess that shut me up. We were driven home and the police spoke to my parents about what happened. Obviously the phone book incident never came up. I had been finger printed, my mug shot taken, the whole nine yards. So did I take the fall? Yes I did, to help a friend, and man, did I ever receive the wrath of my parents for it. I tried to explain my case to them but there was absolutely no hearing of it. I was guilty and that was it. There was nothing more to be said about it. I don't think my parents truly know or believe to this day that I did not steal that cassette.

I would stick up for friends many more times during my lifetime and I would get burned doing it. But for some inexplicable reason, I would just keep doing it again and again and again. Was I stupid?

I remember getting a tattoo at the very young age of fifteen to be original. I hated followers and copy cats and I guarantee there was no other kid like Mark Stewart. My parents would say they broke that mould. I pierced my ears when no one had earrings and everyone said, "Oh God, look at him." I got a grim reaper skull with cross bones on my arm and that was the first real visible beginning of the rebellious stage. I remember telling a friend about the tattoo and showing him. He asked, "What's your Mom going to think?" I answered, "No worries. She's cool." I went home with my new scar and my Mom asked me to sit down and talk to her. So I did. She asked to see my arms. I thought, "WHAT?" She demanded, "Let me see your arm." So I showed her my left arm (my tattoo is on my right arm) and she looked at it, then said, "Ok, now the other one." I lifted my sleeve . . . she said, "Higher." . . . I lifted my sleeve a bit higher. She saw my tattoo and asked me what that was on my arm. I asked her why on earth would she want me to show her my arm for anyway, that she had never done anything like that ever before. She then told me she received a phone call and the person on the other side asked her, "What's the big idea of letting Mark get a tattoo?", to which she responded with, "What the heck are you talking about?" He then said, "OOOPS, I GOT THE WRONG NUMBER." and quickly hung up. So the result was, I got busted by my own friend. So began the progression of my tattoo saga. I added a few more throughout my rebelliousness and then when my girlfriend freaked out on me I added another one, I guess to annoy her. It worked. I have about twenty-two now. I would have liked to cover my arms and back completely but unfortunately as you will find out that will get stopped as well.

HIGH SCHOOL DAZE

High school was a whole new ball of wax for me. Up to this point I seemed to feel in control of my life but for some reason, I don't know what, all hell seemed to break loose inside of me at this time.

This is where I am going to be very honest with everyone, and myself, and not hide anything. It is a release for me to remember my past and acknowledge the truths lurking behind my behaviour and experiences in my life as I move forward. It is a story leading up to my future with Multiple Sclerosis that I feel is necessary to share.

So all you people out there who know me as a gentle, kind person . . . hold on tight (and maybe get another drink).

I was fifteen and starting high school with a chip on my shoulder the size of Brampton (the city I lived in). I was registered at a high school where most of my friends were going and I didn't want to be in some lame brain history class or studying boring, uninteresting geography. At least that was how I felt at the time. I only wanted art, art and more art. I remember having a fight the very first day of school with a grade twelve student and subsequently getting hauled off to the office for discipline. I promptly told them that I wasn't going to stay in the office and wait for the principal. The secretary said to sit and wait. I remember getting up and then leaving to go home but not before saying, "I will never come back to this hole." It took me three days to get out of that school for good. My Mom worked really hard to get me accepted into a new school. Finally, I went to a trade school that was basically for the social outcasts and the bad ass kids, a group I fit right in with. That first day of school I had a fight with another grade twelve student because he had heard of my previous school issues from a friend and he wanted to 'set things straight with me at this school.' I guess he was just trying to put me in my place in the new jungle. No worries. I stood my ground and we ended up becoming good friends later.

I recall a time when I was very young and staying with my Grandfather and Grandmother for a visit. My Grandfather was mugged in his building as he went downstairs for something. He encountered two punks who told him, "White man, give us your wallet.", to which my Grandfather replied. "Like hell I will.", and beat them up Sylvester Stallone (Rocky) style. His picture was in the newspaper shortly after that. He posed like the boxer he was in his early days. I always loved this picture of him and the story behind it. I think I got my fighting attitude and not being afraid of anyone from him. Thanks Grampa!!

I was in grade nine, hanging out with the big boys, and thinking this was great, but peer pressure was about to punch me in the face. I don't follow anyone or do things just because others do, but if I hear you can't or you won't, then I will. I began smoking cigarettes a lot more and even pot was also on the menu several times. I never cared for people that would do harder stuff. I didn't do that myself. It just wasn't for me.

We had dares at school, something like a 'Rite of Passage', that you had to do from which I was not immune. I had to do, and did do, things people wouldn't even have believed. For example, throwing fire crackers into staff room meetings and stealing a basketball during a game, then taking it outside. Yep, I got caught and yep, I took the punishment for it. I remember the smoking area and how, after every class, I would run out, have a cigarette and then sprint into the next class where I would just relax and mellow out. I took four classes, Art, Math, English and a Horticultural class simply because it was an easy credit for me and, more importantly, in close proximity to the smoking area.

School was a just place for me to hang out and be cool. I skipped so many classes I forgot my agenda so I felt I had no choice but to not go back to classes in the afternoons at all. I think I might have missed over two hundred classes that year. I would walk down to a local pool hall where I would meet friends, hang out there and waste my days. Grade ten was pretty much the same routine for me. I had a night job working at the local clubs doing stage setups and sound systems. It paid good money, but it was money I would blow away in no time. I remember some bands asking if they could pay me in marijuana. Sure thing I would say. I was offered hard drugs (cocaine) by a famous artist but was never interested so I stayed away from that payment. I was given beer, alcohol and drugs to do my jobs. So now here I was, fifteen years old—just shy of sixteen, getting about a Hundred Dollars a night to do work and I can never remember going home with any money.

March 14, 1985 was a day I will never forget. My life changed forever that day. I was babysitting for a neighbour. Why me? I have no idea but I was doing just that. I had some friends over with me and we were watching a movie. There was a snow storm outside. Once the movie had ended one of the guys had to go home, it was very bad weather outside and for whatever reason I took the car keys and said we would drive him home.

I left the kids with another neighbour who was available and drove my friend home. BIG MISTAKE!! We were involved in a horrible car crash. The car rolled and one of my passengers was thrown out the back window. My arm was caught outside the car. Thank God I *had my seatbelt on* or I would have quite probably been killed. I wound up breaking my arm and having multiple injuries, but that was the very least of my problems. I was arrested and kept in custody in the hospital, because little to my knowledge, the car was considered stolen. I thought I was helping a friend. See the pattern? I was charged with grand theft auto, dangerous driving, reckless endangerment, destruction of public property and driving without a license or insurance. I could have gone to jail for years but I just got under the wire of the Young Offenders Act by mere days. The Act went into effect on March 10. I turned 16 in February. I had to appear at court and was put on probation for a period of two years. My license was suspended before I even had one. What a mess I had created for myself and everyone involved.

I remember returning to school and being looked and talked about as if I had killed someone. Although it was a pretty close encounter, thank God that didn't happen. I remember people from other schools who prayed for me while I was hospitalized and in recovery and I thought that the prayers would change me for the better, but it wasn't long before the old demon popped his head out again.

A little over a month later, on April 23, 1985 I was involved in another very serious car accident which almost took my life. I was crushed in the back seat of a car driven by a friend. We were definitely speeding and we hit a very large tree head on. I was knocked out cold and the tow truck driver was actually the one that found me. I was taken into the hospital with my leather jacket over my face because I was cut up that badly (not what my parents thought when they saw me being wheeled me in with my face covered). I remember saying Happy Birthday to my Dad when I came to as it was in fact his birthday. He said he got his wish. I was alive. I had suffered severe trauma and pain, crushed vertebrae in my neck (C1 & C2) and had major back problems. The doctors said I even had breaks in my back (this will creep up to haunt me later in life as well). I had lived through another major traumatic incident. I was in a few more smaller accidents in later years that caused some unbelievable pain but none as bad as suffering through the pain of two months in major back to back accidents.

I again returned to school only this time I felt like I was almost invincible. I had just survived two of the most horrific crashes that Brampton had seen. I remember hearing again that people I didn't even know had actually prayed for my recovery.

I want to take this time to say a very heartfelt and grateful thank you for all the prayers that have been sent my way. I don't take them for granted. I know I have been touched by them. Thank you.

Following the last accident, I had to go to a chiropractor every day for about two years as my back was completely damaged and I could barely move. I remember the smell of the office and the table the Doctor would use. I don't honestly think it ever helped me though. I seemed to always hurt. I had tried many different beds, including a waterbed, but my pain and discomfort was so severe that nothing seemed to help and I was not able to sleep well.

Now I was in a deep trouble in my life. I had the car accident with a stolen car, court dates, probation, problems at school and now another car accident that would surely change my life for the worse with my damaging physical issues, not to mention the emotional and mental states I was in. How was I even alive after all this? I still ask that question in my head to this day as what I went through would have surely killed most people.

School was a nightmare for me and I was fast tracking my way out. I took art classes because art was a release for me. I took special graphic art classes and had a hand at painting the walls at my school. I enjoyed this part of my education but it didn't take me long before being in school had that crushing affect on me again. I began to skip classes and I just seemed to stop caring about anything anymore. I would go to my old school during the afternoons (after my art class at noon) to hang out with friends and I would even go into classes with them without being recognized as a student who didn't belong there anymore. This occupied my time and kept me away from the continuing downfall of my schooling. I followed this new routine until the summer arrived.

So it was now the summer of 1986. **Let the party begin!** I hung around a lot of people and got into a lot of nonsense. I was again dating my former girlfriend and was just spending my time wasting my summer away. One of my good friends back then would always call me and ask me to come over and hang out. He had a cousin who lived in Mississauga and when he was there he called me to come over. I agreed, so I got my girlfriend, my cousin, someone he was dating and off we went to my friend's cousin's apartment to get some stuff. While we were there I remember seeing this really pretty girl, but I was not really paying any attention to her as I was with my girlfriend. So after a good visit we left. That girl would come back into my life in a major way later on (and remain there). My summer slipped away like most summers do. Time was spent at concerts, beaches, the gravel pit, hockey, and hanging out with friends.

I was also working at the local clubs doing stage setups and odd jobs to get extra money. I always hated authority and never stayed at a job if I didn't like it. I didn't care what the job was or how much it paid. I once quit a job because a lawnmower pissed me off and I ended breaking that lawnmower before I left. A definite pattern emerged and it continued for a long time. I bounced from job to job and place to place throughout that summer. Summer seemed to go by quickly and before I knew it, I was on my way back to school.

Grade eleven began as usual and I didn't get into any of the classes I wanted. They had me registered for English, Science and 'lame brain' History. I had messed around with my course selections in grade ten and think I said I wanted to major in Lunch and minor in Downhill Skiing (I hate snow but I was just messing around anyway). I guess they fixed my wagon or so they thought. I recall being in a cooking class and thinking, "Man, is this my future? Making freaking french fries in a cafeteria. "No way" I told the teacher I was done and I was going to quit. He said, "I bet you Fifty Dollars you don't have the balls to quit and besides you need your parents consent." I said, "Get your money ready 'cause I'll be back to collect it in twenty minutes." With that, I stormed out of the class as I flipped him the finger, went to the office and said, "I'm done. I QUIT!" The secretary, who was actually nice to me as she had met me many, many times throughout the past couple of years said, "Mark, are you sure this is what you want?" I told her that I was so done with all the BS and I just wanted out. She asked me if I had a plan and I told her I would figure one out. The school called my Mom while I was on the phone with my girlfriend's Father, asking him if I could come to work for him full time. He said yes and then I spoke to my Mom on the phone. She was not happy at all and she said, "What are you going to do during the day? You aren't sleeping all day." I told her I had a job to go to and would be fine. So I quit school and was ready to leave when I remembered that the teacher owed me Fifty Dollars on the bet so I went back to collect. I showed him my walking papers and told him he owed me Fifty Dollars to which he replied, "I don't pay people who quit on themselves." My reply, "I didn't quit on myself. I quit on this school." And there it was, my school was finished for good and I would never look back again. The next day was the first day of the rest of my life. I got up at four-thirty in the morning and took the bus to work. It seemed to take me forever to get there and I was late by an hour. I thought "Oh boy, I'm dead meat.", but my boss told me he would start picking me up and dropping me off at home. So it worked out well for quite a while. I was very good at what I did and was happy having a semblance of normal life, making decent money and doing something I was good at. I enjoyed working with wood and refinishing furniture. I remember my boss always wanting to hang around and have a few beers after work. I was part of the group now too, but I didn't drink with them. I was too young at that time. Thank God, because I probably would have been trashed every day. I stayed employed there for quite some time, even after my girlfriend and I broke up for the final time. We were just two very different people. I was not waiting for anyone and I just hated people telling me what to do. I believe I worked there for about a year before deciding I needed to move on and pursue other avenues of employment, so I quit. I'm writing about this time in my life as just a part of looking back to see what, if any, impact various situations contributed to my becoming so sick. As I review this time in my life, I realize I inhaled so much pollution working day in and day out in a refinishing shop, that it may have had some affect on me too. I would never blame this circumstance or anyone in the refinishing business. This is just another area I wonder about in my looking for some answers. Who knows?

I had changed jobs a few times as I was just not happy in them and if I was not happy I was not about to stick around anywhere. "I didn't care."

THE LOVE OF MY LIFE

January of 1987 would turn out to be the greatest month in my entire life. I remember it so clearly. My good friend at the time called me and said he was coming over and asked if he could bring a friend. I told him yes. Everyone always hung out at my house, so having more company was no problem. He came by in the early afternoon and he had this Goddess with him. She was beautiful stood about 5'4", had dark hair and the most beautiful brown eyes I have ever seen. She was wearing blue eye liner and had on tight blue jeans that hugged a beautifully shaped body, a beige sweater that was kind of revealing and a burgundy leather jacket. She was definitely a Goddess and there she was, standing in my house with me. I remember instantly falling for her. It is so true when they say **"love at first sight"**. It hit me hard and I knew I was in love instantly. I remember saying to my friend, "This is the girl I want to marry." And this is funny because I always said I would never get married or settle down. I was wild, crazy and free and here I am making a commitment in my head to spend my life with someone before I even knew her. We spoke on the phone later in the day and I remember before that call, my friend and I kept saying to each other, she is calling in four hours, she is calling in three hours, she is calling in two hours. Countdown continues. I could not wait for that call. After that we talked every day and went out several times. Arlette and I started officially dating a week later. Life was good and I was so happy. We spent all our time together and enjoyed every minute of each other's company so much, She was my everything. I remember walking to her house to pick her up and walking her home at night to make sure she was safe. If her Dad said to have her home at nine that evening, she was there at ten minutes to nine. She lived about four miles from my house but it meant nothing for me to take her home just so I could spend the extra time with her. I would walk back home by myself and think about the next day and what it would bring. Sometimes my walk got me home close to midnight but time would just seem to pass by with no worries when I was with her.

I remember one time my Mom had driven me to get Arlette from her house. When we got there she had already left and was walking towards my house, so we headed back. We were driving near my house when I spotted her walking along the side walk and I saw some teens riding their bikes towards her so I kept an eye on her. One of the punks decided to grab her from behind and he got a handful. I jumped out of the car even though it was still moving and went after him. I made sure I saw him clearly and would remember that face as I felt like I was going to kill him if I caught him (not actually but figuratively speaking). I did not catch him but I was definitely determined to find him. We returned to my house where I changed, grabbed my bike and away I went. I searched the area where the incident took place and then went to the local store just to check it out. There he was, with his friends. I pulled him off his bike, pounded him into a brick wall and punched him until my hand hurt. Then he fell and I kicked at him. I told him that's what you get for grabbing at someone and especially my girlfriend. I was so angry. Nobody, not even his friends, stepped in to help him. He was mine to do with what I wanted. I walked to my bike and rode home. I went in and told Arlette it was taken care of. I'm sure he never grabbed at anyone again. I knew I would protect Arlette at any cost and this was only the beginning.

We were going out for about five months when my parents announced we were moving to Saskatchewan. I said, "WTF?!!! What do you mean we're moving?" I was devastated and didn't know what to do. I was going to lose her. The girl of my dreams is going to be gone because we are moving to the freaking prairies. We talked about this move several times and decided we would work it out somehow. Well, in June my parents did it. We moved to Moose Jaw, Saskatchewan. This was the longest drive of my life and I believe I cried all the way there. I remember stopping at a truck stop and buying a small stuffed toy, writing a letter on it and mailing it to Arlette. This was my dream girl and I was mailing a stuffed toy to tell her I loved her and missed her so much. We hadn't even been apart for two days and I was already so miserable. I knew this was not going to be good. I thought after all the things I had been through in my life, the hard times and the hassles, the headaches, the drama and the near death experiences and then I meet this great girl who has single-handedly changed my outlook on life and now we are leaving her behind. I spent the whole trip trying to figure out what I was going to do without her near me. We arrived in Moose Jaw two days later and not only was I miserable, I now felt a downfall coming on. I started to unpack my things but was very upset and just felt this was not going to work for me. I had to figure out a way to see her again. I had called her when we arrived and not long after that call I decided I was not sticking around in Moose Jaw without her. I remember I had kept a gym bag full of my clothes and a few of my favourite cassettes sitting on my room floor, but I didn't have a plan yet. I just knew I had to get out of Dodge (being Moose Jaw, Saskatchewan), not thinking of what was going to happen when I got back to Toronto. I didn't care if I didn't have a place to go to. I was going to be with Arlette again and damn it I did it. I booked a flight the next morning which my parents paid for. I didn't care what happened to me. I was going home even if it did mean I was going to be homeless. Well, that would definitely end up biting me in the rear. I left Saskatchewan the next day and there I was, heading back to Toronto after spending less than three days away from Arlette.

During the plane flight all I kept thinking about was what I was going to do when I got there. I pictured this fairy tale life and how it was going to be like old times (or at least like a week earlier). Actually, when I had stepped onto the plane in Moose Jaw I was really scared of what was going to happen with me once I did arrive in Toronto. Yes, I was concerned! Could I end up homeless?

I remember landing in Toronto and lying on the luggage rack that was going round and round in circles, while I was waiting for my bags, and just watching the lights on the ceiling go by. My good friend was there at the airport to pick me up and Arlette was with him. I remember seeing her face light up and it was like the most magical feeling I ever had. I was home with my baby and everything would work out. I didn't have a place to stay or call home but that was all right because here I was, with Arlette and that was all that mattered to me. Everything would work out for the good. I had faith.

Well, as it happens, I slept in a park that night on a bench and I remember thinking to myself, "Oh man, I don't think I REALLY expected this!" although it was indeed a worst case scenario that I had briefly given thought to in my bravado and accepted in theory. But now, here I was, actually living it. Reality set in. "OMG . . . yep, I am officially homeless!" With that I curled up on the park bench and went to sleep. Happy! I was with Arlette again.

The next day we hung out and I was planning on what I was going to do, but who was I kidding. I had no clue what I was going to do or where I was going to stay. I took Arlette home as I always did and stayed as long as possible with her so it would not be such a long night in the park for me, which I now called my new home.

I was walking aimlessly in the downtown area and started heading to where I used to live, not sure why, but I wound up there. I curled up on the steps and went to sleep. I woke up in the early morning to find my startled neighbour standing over me, thinking to herself I'm sure, 'What happened? Did his parents leave him here when they left last week?" She asked me those questions. I told her what I had done and how I was now homeless and not sure what to do next. She told me I could stay with them and we would figure it out from there. So that was that. I was no longer homeless. I had a place to stay and was so excited to be able to tell

Arlette that everything was going to be all right. I remember walking all the way to her place to tell her the news and was I feeling good. Wish we had cell phone or texting back then since I could hardly wait to share this with her. I was staying in the basement on some sort of sofa bed which was softer than a park bench or a stairwell plus I had a blanket. Talk about gratitude? I had it.

I started to look for a job so I would have money and also to pay rent. I applied at a truck rental company and remember telling them I could drive a truck, no problems. I remember the first day I saw the gear shift and going WTF? But I figured it out. You have to remember my license was suspended for a few years because of my accident so I didn't have a chance to learn to drive a standard (I watched my Dad driving the truck and that was what saved me. Visual training!) I was hired and did very well at the job. I remember walking to and from work every day in my work boots and wishing I hadn't screwed up my life so badly.

I made Assistant Manager in no time at the job and loved working with my boss. He was great. I was happy, I had my baby back and life was good for me again. I decided that I was going to ask Arlette to marry me and we would take our next step into our future together. She meant everything to me and I wanted to spend my life with her. I planned it for a while and saved my money so I could get her a beautiful ring. I remember going into the store and telling the girl what I was doing. I looked at about fifteen rings and said I was going to give it some more thought. I knew I was going to propose. I just didn't know which ring I wanted for her. But I knew it had to be the perfect ring. I went back and looked at ten of the rings I had in my mind, then walked away again. I returned to look at five of the rings I was leaning towards and then, yep you guessed it, I walked away again, having settled on the final choice to be between two rings I really liked. I returned, sat with the girl and finally decided on the perfect ring for my baby. Then I did it, I bought the ring. Now I was broke big time and thinking how can I do this? I'm going to propose to the girl of my dreams and pray she says yes. I didn't have any money left and no real plans for life, but I knew I wanted to spend it with her no matter what. Well, I asked her to marry me one year to the day that we had met (January 28, 1988) and I actually proposed to her in my new basement room. (It wasn't the romantic proposal I wanted but it was the best I had to offer.)

SHE SAID "YES"

I was the happiest man in the world and thought nothing could go wrong for the rest of my life with me having my angel by my side. I was going to marry her. Life was going to work out for me. The kid that had issues with everybody and everything throughout his entire life, the fights, schools, jobs, and all the other things I failed at were now behind me. I was finally going to be a husband and have a new beginning. We decided to approach the future slowly, making sure we wanted the same thing and were doing it right. I remember a short while later asking Arlette to do the biggest thing she ever did. I asked her to move to Saskatchewan with me. Wow, that was the hardest thing I had ever done. I was asking her to leave her family to go to a place I had left to be with her. My Uncle was a very successful business man in Moose Jaw and I thought we would make it fine. Needless to say and as you can expect, her parents were very upset at her decision to move away, and I don't blame them. But we decided to go, so I went in and quit the job that I loved, explaining that this was a chance at a lifetime for Arlette and I and we were going for it.

We booked our trip on a Greyhound bus and headed out west. Three long days later we arrived in Moose Jaw, Saskatchewan and so began another chapter in our life. It turned out to be a lot harder than we expected. I was able to get part time work through an agency and Arlette worked at my Uncle's gas station. I slugged eighty pound bags of flour in a bakery ten hours a day (I'm sure that did wonders for my neck) and Arlette worked midnight shifts at a gas station. I was not happy to see her working midnights and remember she would call me or I would go over to stay with her. She even had a guy watch out for her while she worked the long nights. It was nuts.

We bought our first car, a 1973 Monte Carlo, for Seven Hundred and Fifty Dollars and were trying to make it on our own. Remember my license had been suspended in Ontario as a result of my car incident? I found a loop hole that would allow me to get my license in Saskatchewan so I went for it. I took my driving test in my car (the Monte Carlo) and the instructor was questionable to me to say the least. Physically he was near 6'4" and weighed about two hundred and sixty pounds. Definitely a big guy. I did my first test in the Monte Carlo. He told me to go the wrong way on a one way street. OK! Well, I hit a garbage can while attempting to parallel park. It was too small of an area to manoeuvre such a large car, and apparently I squealed the tires at a stop sign—accidently. I was failed and told to try again in two weeks. I tried to blame him since he told me to go the wrong way, then told me to park in that tiny space, and I even tried to blame the peel out on him, but to no avail. I returned two weeks later and I was still annoyed with the instructor. I came to my test with my Grandmother's car. It was a 1977 Honda Civic (about the size of a mini). I barely fit in it and I knew he wouldn't for sure. He tried to squeeze his way into the car and I told him he had better buckle up. He could not even get the seatbelt on. We drove around the corner and before long he told me to STOP! He passed me on the spot. So now I was licensed.

I remember a time when we were in Moose Jaw, I was having some issues with my back and we went to see a specialist. We did some tests and he came back and said we could consider surgery but there is only a fifty-fifty chance. We said, "Of walking?" He said, "No, of living through it." We opted out of that surgery.

I remember my Dad was on a road trip and Toronto was one of his stop-overs. My Mom decided to go for a visit there and then drive back in the truck with him. During her visit to Toronto, I found a small apartment for Arlette and myself. It was cute and reasonably priced, but we had no furniture and no extra money to furnish it. I remember taking all of my Mom's furniture from their basement and whatever else I needed. I fully furnished our new apartment. My Mom returned from her trip and I told her to come see our new home right away. She was very excited that her kid finally had his own place. She walked in and said, "What the heck? Boy, does this ever look like my place." She had not stopped off at her home first from her trip, so it was news to her that I taken her furniture for my place. "She surely wasn't going to take it back." Ha! Ha! Ha!

So now we had a place to live, jobs and a fresh life but it somehow wasn't feeling right. I could sense every day that Arlette was not happy. She finally came to me sometime around May or June and said her sister was going to have her first baby and she wanted to go back home to be there for when he was born. It bothered me but we agreed she would leave and I would stay and then head back to Toronto as well, as soon as I could.

My nephew was born in July that year and Arlette was not with me. Once again I had a wall holding me back and I needed to figure out a way to knock it down. I remember a time that my past would even come to haunt me while I was in Saskatchewan. I remember a knock on my door and this guy in a suit asking, "Are you Mark Stewart?" I told him yes and asked who he was. He told me he was a private investigator hired by the courts to find me because I had left Ontario illegally. The accident was still chasing after me. I didn't realize I wasn't supposed to leave Ontario. I think my Mom must have sorted it out somehow as I don't remember him ever coming back after that.

I stayed for a while longer then sold the car and furniture. I was leaving for Toronto to be with my fiancé. I recall booking a plane ticket and getting all my belongings together to organize myself for my flight home. I was watching the news on the morning of my flight when I heard there had been an emergency landing in Vancouver for a Toronto bound flight. Yep! That was my flight. I freaked out thinking this might be some kind of bad omen and maybe something didn't want me back in Toronto. I asked my Mom to take me to the train station to see what was available. We went to the Via Rail booth to find out what was Toronto bound for the week. We were told one train was leaving in two hours. I panicked. I wasn`t ready to leave in two hours! My flight had been booked for a six o'clock evening departure and it was just eleven in the morning. I didn't have much time to get ready for the train departure in two hours but I booked it anyway and went home to grab my stuff. I quickly packed a bag with clothes and a magazine I loved, then headed right back to the train station and jumped on board the train for Toronto. My Mom called Arlette and explained what happened, I believe, and arranged for me to be picked up at Union Station in Toronto. Everything happened so fast.

The train ride was two and a half days long so I had plenty of time to think and lots of time to drink, which I did. I also played cards with some guys going to Sudbury. I remember stopping in Winnipeg and going around Lake Superior. It was beautiful, but I probably would have appreciated it more if I hadn't been trashed. I remember coming into Toronto around seven in the evening and Arlette's Dad was there to pick me up. OH GOD, I thought he was going to kill me. Here I was still half buzzed from the train ride and had just wasted over Three Hundred Dollars on a flight which I never even took. We had a good talk in the car and I assured him I was going to treat Arlette right. I think that helped. We stayed with her sister and her boyfriend (who would eventually become my brother-in-law) and my new nephew. We got our own place shortly after that and started another chapter in our life.

I remember hearing from someone that while I was away a so-called friend of mine hit on Arlette and said while Mark is away and what Mark doesn't know won't hurt him. Well it did. I found him and needless to say, a beating ensured. Won't hurt huh? Mark was back and trouble was started already.

We had moved into our own place and then decided to let some friends stay with us to help them out. That back fired though as they ended up destroying our house, leaving us to pay for the damages. We never expected this to happen to us when we decided to give some assistance to people who were in need. Lessons!!

I also remember we moved into an apartment on our own that was right next door to Arlette's sister. So in the span of about two and a half years I had made about four major moves and had moved across Canada twice.

I returned to my old job and settled in quickly, so we thought we were off to a great start again. On we went with our lives. We were both very happy to be back where we belonged. I remember Arlette going on a trip to Mexico one year with a friend and I decided to have a party at our house while she was away (approved by Arlette). I arranged for a few of my heavy-set friends to be the security and for a cousin, who was a black belt in martial arts, to make sure nothing happened or got broken. We bought a few kegs of beer and partied for six days straight. I remember playing video games, drinking, drinking, more drinking and even having beer in my Fruit Loops for breakfast (gross). We stayed awake for almost four days. It was quite a party but nothing got broken, not even one glass. We did have to get more beer though. Arlette came home and we were back to normal in no time. We lived in that house for about two years and then I remember my parents had decided to come back to Toronto as well. They returned in 1991.

I remember one day Arlette was at work and I was home alone. I was walking down our hallway when I suddenly collapsed and couldn't breathe. I wasn't sure what was happening. I thought I was having a heart attack and I was only twenty-one. OMG! I called my Mom as she was a nurse years before and she was good at diagnosing problems quickly with me. She thought it was gas but said she would take me to the doctor's office just in case. When we got there the Doctor took his stethoscope and checked my chest. His mouth dropped wide open and he told my Mom to get me to Emergency right away. He didn't even take a second to explain what was wrong to me. He said something to my Mom that she understood immediately. She rushed me to the Emergency right away and somehow got in touch with Arlette. She told her that my lung had collapsed and it was urgent that she get to hospital right away. I remember the Doctor putting a huge needle in my side and being in excruciating pain and then a numb sort of feeling and him asking me if I could feel it. I told him I could feel something but wasn't sure what it was. I wasn't about to look either. Needles are not my good friends. It was apparently his hand in my chest trying to open my lung that was causing the unusual sensation I was feeling. I was hooked up to a ventilator for a week and it would now breathe for me. I decided then and there that my life needed a new direction and I stopped smoking and drinking. However, it seems that wouldn't last long.

I returned to work and things started to go downhill with the new management. I felt they were starting to take advantage of me and the numbers of hours I was working. I was putting in twelve hours a day, five days a week and they wanted more. I told the new boss I wasn't going to do it. He said he was going on holidays and we would talk when he got back. I told him, "If you leave before we settle this, I'm quitting." He didn't believe me and left.

When I say something I make sure I'm right and if I'm wrong I will be the first to admit it, but when I say something I MEAN it. He went on his holiday and I notified head office that I was leaving. They begged me to stay and told me they would fix it. They didn't do anything and I knew my health had to come first. So when the new boss returned from his holiday and said he needed a couple more days to be ready for work, I told him to be at work in one hour or I would lock the door, send my employees home and I would walk out. He didn't come . . . I WALKED OUT . . . flipped a finger to the place and never looked back. I eventually went back to school for my college degrees in order to secure a future for Arlette and I. I graduated with very good grades in accounting, business and computers.

Arlette had started to plan the wedding and I remember we were going to get married in a Catholic church and I was far from being a Catholic. We were going to get married at a church that Arlette had attended when she was in school. We had to attend a meeting to talk to the Priest about what we could do because I wasn't Catholic. I was really nervous but we arranged to talk to the Priest. We had to also do it separately for some reason and I guess this was their way to ensure we were making the right decision.

I remember him lecturing me about my tattoos and stating my hair was too long and he didn't see us working out and then he had the nerve to tell Arlette I was not good enough for her and she shouldn't marry me. Wow! (All we can say is after twenty-four plus years together we are still going strong.) I was so upset by this whole thing that I said I wanted to get married in a park. Arlette said we would go to another church and we didn't need this Priest. I agreed so we met with a Deacon since I wasn't of the Catholic faith which meant we would not be permitted to have a Priest marry us.

We talked to the Deacon and we felt very comfortable with him performing our wedding.

I remember the Deacon said we needed to attend marriage classes before we got married. I was again very nervous about this as I have never been good with people telling me what to do and how to do it. We attended the classes and did quite well. We met some very nice people while taking the classes. We received our Certificate of Completion and were now set to get married. Arlette started the planning of our wedding again and she did an amazing job. It was beautiful to see her so happy making the arrangements. I remember I was looking for a limousine for our wedding. I had gone to a car show and saw the car I wanted for my baby on our special day. It was a 1955 Cadillac, white and gorgeous beyond words. I asked the owner if he would provide his car and services for our wedding. He replied it was only a show car and he didn't do weddings. I was devastated but I don't take to 'no' to well, so I asked him again and said I would pay anything to have my wife arrive in this car. He said, 'No!' again. Well I asked him about fifteen times but to no avail, so I returned the next day to the car show with a stool and sat beside him, then asked, "Will you do my wedding?" He replied with his own question, "Are you going to sit here and do this all day to me?" to which I responded, "You bet I am." Finally he agreed he would do it and said he never met anyone so determined and aggressive to get what he wants. I told him, "I'm Mark Stewart and you have just made my day." With that, I booked our Limo. I did not tell anyone about this car. It was so amazing because not only was this car beautiful but it had belonged to James Dean before his death. Can you believe it? I got a car that was owned by a Hollywood legend for my wedding. I was so excited. It was set. I had everything I wanted for that day, but something would happen to throw a wrench into the whole thing. I wrote my speech with my Grandfather who I thought the world of. He was sick, in the hospital and wasn't doing very well. I remember going over my speech at his bedside and him saying, "That's nice." or change this or that. My Grandfather died two weeks before my wedding so I had to re-write the entire speech as it now had a totally different meaning to me.

Our Wedding Day

Arlette worked non-stop and outdid herself for us to have a gorgeous wedding to remember. And it was a beauty, one never to be forgotten! September 26, 1992 was our day. We were going to the chapel and we were going to get married.

Her parents and sisters flew in from Malta (where they had moved). I remember the night before my wedding my new brother-in-law got me so drunk playing bottle caps that I almost didn't make it to the wedding sober. We got up at five in the morning and I think I had slept for maybe ten minutes. I remember getting ready and going to my parents house for photos and being out of it. I sobered up real quick and we did our photos. We even had a laugh as we were alternately trying to leave and trying to run back in the house for more photo shoots.

I would have run all the way to the church as I was so excited to marry the girl of my dreams, but I was definitely beyond scared. Was I good enough for her? This question was in my head a lot after the Priest, who we had met in the beginning to discuss our plans to marry, had said I wasn't good enough for Arlette. He was concerned I had tattoos and long hair, and he felt he couldn't see it working out for us. This stuck with me for a long time and sometimes I still wonder and ask myself that same question. I guess he did not expect us to make it very far, but we have just had our twenty-fourth year together in January so that speaks for itself I think.

"Back to our wedding day" We arrived at the church and I was so nervous about seeing my bride-to-be. We stood up at the front waiting for my bride and the Deacon suggested that I should just look upwards so I wouldn't cry while she was walking down the aisle. She had arrived and I could hear people talking about the car. I looked upwards and saw Jesus on the wall. I said hi to Him and asked Him to wish us luck and then began to count the tiles on the ceiling. I was so focused on my counting that I didn't even see Arlette coming down the aisle until the very last minute when I looked to see where she was. OH MY GOD!! She was beautiful. I often say she is two wings shy of being an angel and that day she truly was. She looked incredible (and still does).

The wedding ceremony was very nice and then the Deacon said that magic sentence, "I now pronounce you Husband and Wife." We had done it—we were married. I remember my Mom signalling with her mouth, **"IT'S TOO LATE."** She was definitely talking to Arlette because I was in heaven and I had just married the woman of my dreams.

We went outside for photos and the limo driver was there with our chariot. He had a red carpet rolled out, was wearing a top hat, a black suit and carrying a cane. He even had a beautiful sign that said "**Just Married**". Man, he went all out and it was amazing. Oh my God, it was so beautiful and we were married, so now onto the party. We had drinks in the limo and went for photos of ourselves, and the family at Gage Park.

We went to our reception and had a great night of family fun, dancing and drinking. I remember how difficult it was for me to give my speech because of the recent death of my Grandfather. And, we also had an announcement!! Arlette and I were moving to Malta. **"SURPRISE!"**

We managed to get through the evening and we decided to invite my sister-in-law and family up to our hotel room as they were here from Europe for just a short while and we would have the next night and the rest of our lives for ourselves. My brother-in-law and I drank some more while sitting in the hot tub and stuck beer labels on the tiled wall of the hot tub. We filled that wall up throughout the night. I think we finally went to bed when the sun came up. I remember my four year old nephew came in, woke me up and asked me to sit in the hot tub with him. He did such as great job as our ring bearer and had so much fun at the wedding. I told him to fill it up and I would go in with him. Then I drifted back into my coma-like state of sleep. He came back a little while later and told me he was ready. I jumped up, yelled, "**BONZAI**", ran across the room and jumped into an **ice cold** hot tub. He had filled it with freezing cold water. You can bet I was more than awake at that point.

Arlette and I didn`t go on a honeymoon because we now had to save for our move to Europe and we would be starting over again. I remember we stayed at our apartment for a while before moving to Europe. I also remember we were at my parent's place and my Mom telling us she was getting a little girl to look after so she had to go to the store to get some items for her arrival. (My parents were and still are foster parents). While she was out the doorbell rang and a social worker came in with this beautiful little girl and we were there to greet her with open arms. That was in December, just before Christmas. So we had another little girl in the family and then on February 19, my birthday, the little girl's brother also came to live with us. So now we had two more little ones in our lives, but Arlette and I wouldn't be here to watch them grow as we were on our way to Europe. I will talk more about them later.

I remember a time a few months before our wedding when my Dad came to me with a request that he and my Mom had received. My biological father had been trying to see me for years. I had always said no. I had no interest in this at all as I had a father I was close to and I didn't feel I needed another one. My Dad suggested I give him a chance and that he just wanted to be friends. I asked him if he was ok with this and my Dad said he was. I finally agreed to meet my biological father for the first time in almost twenty years.

Our first meeting was quite awkward as I was very apprehensive about this, although I must admit I had been curious to see what he would have to say and where he was in his life at that point. The meeting went well and we are quite close now as good friends. I never asked what happened between him and my Mom because this was their issue not mine. It has never come up and I will never ask. He has moved on with his life and so have I. He has another son which I was able to meet once but have not seen since. He didn't come to the wedding as I felt that would have been awkward. I also wasn't able to spend much time with him before or after as we were planning our wedding and subsequent move to Malta so our relationship would be put on hold yet again for years.

THE MALTA MOVE

It was February, 1992 when we left for another new start in our life. So in five short years we had moved several times, changed jobs, moved across the country, returned, had the many problems with friends, dealt with my lung collapse, and all the other issues we had, plus two new children being brought into the family and now here we were heading for our new home in Malta, feeling like we were leaving all our problems behind us. I was happily married to the greatest woman in the world and on my way to Europe. Europe? What the heck? I had never been to Europe!! Were they ready for me? I know I was so very excited to make this major move. I remember the day of the flight. I remember being on the plane and as we had just taken off I told Arlette I hoped we would be able to see the Skydome from where we were. It was fairly new and I thought it would look great from the air. The plane took an immediate turn to the left and we saw the dome getting closer. I was able to take an amazing photo of the Toronto Skydome (now the Rogers Centre) and thought, "Cool, something cool already." We went through London, England on our way to Malta and that was totally amazing to me. We were able to see the Concord. I remember having a beer at four o'clock in the morning at the bar in the airport. (I thought to myself, "It's five o'clock somewhere.") Our next flight left at noon London time and we arrived in Malta at three o'clock in the afternoon Malta time. I remember looking down at the ground as we were landing and saying we must be in Libya for fuel or something and Arlette telling me we were 'home'. I could not see windows and the houses looked totally different than what I was used to. I had never ever seen any pictures of Malta before we moved, but I do know I was very excited to get out of Canada. We had to walk directly out of the airplane onto the runway, then to a bus and finally to the airport. I thought we were in Bedrock. We walked into the airport and I fell in love instantly. It was so beautiful, full of marble and it just felt so welcoming. My in-laws and Arlette's cousins, aunts and uncles met us there. We picked up our bags and we were home! "Our new home in Malta".

We walked out of the airport and were embraced by beautiful warm weather. I felt totally at ease. Plus here we are in February and it's warm? Yeah, I can handle this. The whole family had arrived to meet us. It was so nice to see all the relatives again. Then we got into the car. WTF? The steering wheel was on the wrong side and not only that, they drove like complete lunatics. My brother-in-law drove us home and quite frankly I didn't think we were going to make it, but we did (I grew to trust his driving). He was always crazy but it actually turned out he was a good driver and this was just normal European driving. I remember we pulled up to this gorgeous home which was all decked out in marble and had a brass gate.

We went in and settled down. Then my brother-in-law brought me my first Maltese beer and a whole new world opened up. I remember wanting to go explore my new home almost immediately. The next day we went to meet family members and relatives again and I had another Maltese beer. Ohh ohh! A pattern was forming. I decided a couple of days upon our arrival that I was going to venture out on my own and then find my way home, so I jumped on a bus and away I went. I made my way to the capital city of Valletta, promptly found a bar and ordered a beer. The guy said ten cents. I freaking near fell off the chair and immediately said, "Two more please." I walked around a flea market with my drink and when I finished I made my way home. I did what I set out to do. Without getting lost!

I remember going for my Work Book so I could be employed in Malta. I was also trying to learn Maltese. My first words were, "Hello, how are you?—Kif int." and "Thank you.—Grazzi." I even tried to say "Thank you very much", which would be "Grazzi hafna". I practised and practised. I went to get my documents signed at the Government office and remember saying to the man in charge "Grazzi Ohxon" having mistakenly confused it with the correct word "hafna". Apparently I said to person who would endorse my employment existence in Malta, "Thanks Fatso." Nice start Mark and funny enough my language barrier seemed to get worse before it got better. I had bus drivers chase me off buses for calling them derogatory words, swore at store clerks and even once said one of the worst phrases in Maltese in front of the Grandparents. Nice, eh? Not!

I asked my Mother-in-law to only speak to me in Maltese so I could learn the language properly or so I thought. She had her fun with it as well with me. She would tell me to repeat after her, Fork=furketta, Spoon=mgharfa (marfa), Knife=sikkina and she would add Hmar = Donkey which, when I would say it, she would say, "Bhal Ommok.", which means "like your Mother" and laugh. So you see, I had my hands full but I was determined to learn the language.

I must jump back a little bit and reflect on the second day we were in Malta. We had just met the neighbours and they seemed like a nice couple. They asked us if we wanted to go to a club for some drinks and dancing. I was no dancer but give me drinks and you count me in. We went to a nice club with loud dance music, sat at a table and were just relaxing. Arlette asked me to dance with her. So we were dancing and having a good time when this fellow decides to do the Lambada dance with my wife's backside, right in front of me. Not cool, Dude! I moved Arlette's head to the left slightly and proceeded to drill my right hand straight to his face. He fell to the floor. He got back up, looked directly at me and went to get his friends. We went back to our table and just sat there. Next thing you know, he comes up to the table and says, "YOU! Let's go." I jumped up and said to my new neighbour, "Let's go. We're going to have a fight." He backed his way out by saying he was sorry but he didn't fight. There I was, standing by myself and looking at these four guys who were wanting to fight me. I said, "Let's go! I'll fight you all myself." At that moment I was wishing my brother-in-law was with me because I knew he would have been right there beside me (that was one thing about him—he always had my back). I started to head towards the doors so I could fight them outside. I guess when they realized that I was not backing down and I was going to fight them all, the main guy came over to me, said he was sorry and didn`t want to fight me. So here I was in a new country and ready to be in a fight on my second day there. GREAT START. It unfortunately did not stop there. I was in three fights in the first month.

I started my new job and was now ready for my new life. I remember my first day at the office and a lady came to me wanting to know how I liked my breakfast. I told her, "In my belly." She gave me a strange look. She didn't get it. She made me toast and a coffee and I thought, "Wow, they make breakfast for us. Ahhh, the good life." I was hired in the accounting department and doing very well. The boss was leaving for holidays and asked if I would watch over one of his sections of the company. It was a packaging plant that we had and I said sure. Well, I decided to make some changes while he was away and moved some of the employees around. When he returned he asked me what happened and I told him that I thought profits would go up if some changes were made in certain areas. It made sense, they looked into it and found that profits would improve and by over thirty-five percent. Next thing I knew they promoted me to the position of Managing Director of the plant and said I could run it my way. I ran it well, but always thought it could be better if it was upgraded and had better machines. But we didn't ever have the budget for those improvements. I remember I would tell the employees they could do what they needed to do as long as their work got done and got done well. They could take one and a half hours for lunch or leave early, as long as my quota was met or exceeded. It was very well accepted that this foreigner, Mark Stewart, was very fair and did a lot for the guys he worked with. I never considered myself the boss. I would work with them, get dirty with them and lift boxes with them. Some of these boxes were one hundred pounds each. I remember one day lifting a box, my legs buckling with the weight and my entire body going numb. I fell to the floor and thrashed around like an epileptic fish out of water. My body was shaking but I couldn't feel anything. One of my guys ran upstairs to get help and I remember a girl from the office came in to see me. I was put in the car and taken home. They don't think the way we do here in Canada in our work force. This incident happened to me at work and I get a ride home, not taken to the hospital.

When I arrived at home my wife had to take me to Emergency. I was put on traction as they thought it was my neck that compressed causing my body to collapse. The traction gadget shifted causing me to choke and I couldn't get it off, so there I was, hanging myself. I finally managed, to break the strap and get myself out of it. I freaked out on the Doctor and asked him what in the world it was that he had just done to me. Unbelievable! I was released two days later and never found out what it was that had happened. All I knew was that I was out of the place they called a hospital and I was happy.

I went back to work a few days later and never gave that collapse another thought. Little did I know it would pay a visit to me again later on in my life.

I remember we bought our first family car, a **FIAT UNO**. I think that translated in English to "**F**ix **I**t **A**gain **T**ony (F.I.A.T.)**. I'm sure many people drive Fiat's and enjoy them but my personal experience started off bad. I remember driving this brand new car off the lot (yes, it was brand new) and discovering the brakes didn't work. WTF? I went back into the dealership and asked, "Did you see that? No brakes!" It turned out the brakes had been installed wrong. Good start.

I remember a short time later that my company had started to lose money in other areas of the company and we were going out of business fast. They needed to take some action to curb their expenses. I remember the boss telling me that they decided to close my section down, running it only when they needed too. I was the only section that made a profit and they were closing us!! Hello! I knew we were in trouble from that day on. I started to work up in the freezers helping load orders for the trucks. I remember driving the large trucks and doing the deliveries. I was the only driver that was able to back the trucks up properly and get them into cities where no one else could. I remember taking a twenty-seven foot truck into a city they called the Silent City (Mdina) I was going to round a very sharp corner so I hit the horn to let oncoming traffic know there was a large truck coming. Not a good thing to do as I got in trouble with the police on patrol. They said the truck was too big for the city and horns were not allowed to be used. They made me back out nearly eight hundred feet through the narrow streets and make the delivery by hand. I did that and completed my deliveries. I returned the next day in my truck and did my deliveries with no problems this time. They said the truck was too big but maybe they had just never seen a driver do it before without crashing into anything. So now I became the driver for the difficult deliveries and the weird locations. I remember a hotel that we serviced where you had to back up the street, then down and into the driveway. It was challenging enough to do it driving forward in a car and here I was expected to do it with a twenty-seven foot long truck—backwards! I got my driving ability from my Dad I'm sure because I did it with absolutely no issues. Take that! So I was considered to be an "A Class" driver and was asked to do deliveries. I did that job for a while and would help wherever anyone needed assistance. I remember preparing my truck for a huge delivery day. I was in the freezer getting my order ready. This is an industrial freezer nearly four thousand square feet in size and about eighty feet high that was stacked with boxes of frozen meats. I was loading one hundred cases of steaks and had to climb up the racks of boxes to get my orders where the fork lift couldn't reach. The forklift operator lifted me about thirty feet up in the air and I climbed onto the boxes to load the pallet onto the forklift. I must have miss-stepped because the boxes shifted and down I went, right off the side and aaallll the way down. I landed on a steel pallet with railings which I hit right on the side with my chest and then I bounced up from the impact. Oh my God! I screamed as I was in so much pain (well I actually yelled something else but it is called profanity). I broke four ribs and cracked one. A thirty foot fall and hitting a steel pallet. Are you kidding me? I returned to work three days later, but couldn't do much of anything because the pain in my chest was excruciating. I did some order runs and set up some deliveries.

This did not last too long and then the bosses told me that I would be laid off soon as the company was going to file for bankruptcy. My ribs had healed and I began searching for another job so when it came time for my lay off I would be already prepared. I worked for that company for almost three years and then this happens. I had made some amazing friends with my colleagues and even had some funny adventures. I went out drinking with my friend and decided to leave my car a distance from the bar where we wound up. We went from bar to bar and got trashed. I asked if he would drive me to my car. We headed out and not three minutes later we rear ended a car. My friend told the guy since there was no damage he should just leave, which he did. We drove a little further along and bang, we hit the same guy a second time. He got out again and my friend told him, once more, to just go away and the guy did. Wow! Can you believe we hit him again, the third hit, only this time he didn't even get out of his car. He just drove ahead and turned a corner so he wasn't near us anymore. My friend dropped me off at my car. I drove home in no higher than third gear because I had been drinking heavily. I was driving slowly knowing full well that I had made a mistake and should never have driving in the first place. Amazingly I made it home. But no more drinking adventures with my friend. Oh wait, yes there was. We went fishing from a huge cliff with a few of our friends. I remember parking at the top and asking what were we supposed to do here? They said we would climb down into the cave and fish from there. This cave seemed like it was nearly two hundred feet high and I knew my fishing rod would not make it to the water. Then we started drinking. A few beers later I started to fish. My rod went flying right out of my hand on my first cast and straight into the water, so no more fishing for me. My friend started a fire for cooking and then he started banging some pots and began dancing. Suddenly all these bats started to fly out of the cave. I hit the ground so fast and we laughed so hard. We had a barbeque and drank—a lot. We stayed there most of the night and luckily we did not get in trouble when we got home. On another trip we did manage to catch an eel.

I remember golfing in Malta with my brother-in-law and having such a laugh it should have been in a movie. Who would think that a dozen beers on a hot day and a golf ball could cause so much chaos. I hit a tree two feet away from me and that ball came back faster then it went forward that's for sure. I broke my nine iron around a tree and I hit a car in the parking lot with a bad shot. We played golf a number of times and had a great time each time we played. We played baseball together on a team of mostly Canadians and had great times again. My brother-in-law was a catcher and I was third baseman as well as centre field. I will talk about more fun times later because there were plenty of them.

I also remember a time when I was having the issues with my neck that I had experienced earlier. I made an appointment to see an acupuncture specialist and was driving to the appointment. (This was a few months after we bought our new car, a Mazda 323F).

I was on my cell phone and this is frowned upon in Malta. I spotted a cop on a motorcycle coming towards me. The road was narrow so I pulled over between two cars on my passenger side to let him pass and I put my phone on my lap so he wouldn't see it. He passed me and we both went on our way. I went to the see the Doctor for my acupuncture which I was not fond of having. The needles hurt and irritated me and I was very uncomfortable going through this process. I went home as soon as I was finished. My wife was going out so she left our son, who was about six months old, with me.

I heard a knock at the door, picked up my son and went to see who it was. There were two cops standing at my door. They asked me if I was Mark Stewart and I told them I was. Then one of them told me they had come to arrest me. WHAT? Then he proceeded to tell me I was being arrested for an attempted hit and run on a police officer. I asked him if he was crazy. He asked me, "Were you here at this place at this time?" to which I responded with a yes and I told him I saw the cop and I had moved over for him. The other cop started to look over my car and then I got upset. I told him to get away from the car or he was going to have a serious problem.

I didn't want anyone touching my car. It had been modified by a local car care centre and I loved it. It was called FROSTBITE (my nickname) and our plates were 'WLD-323'. I had asked for 'FA-Q-2' but they didn't allow it. Not sure why as it meant

'Flashy-And-Quick-2'. Lol.

Back to the story.

My neighbour heard the commotion and came out of his house to see what was going on so now I had a witness and I let the cops have it big time. I yelled at them in my broken Maltese as my neighbour only understood a bit of English. I told the officer I will put my son down and beat the *** out of the other cop if he touched my car. The cop then started to talk down to me and I told him to just shut up and to take off his badge so we could find out just how tough he was. I was so angry now it wasn't funny. We yelled back and forth for a bit and I was very rude with him. The one cop took out his handcuffs and I asked what he was planning to do. He stepped back as my neighbour came over and yelled at them. They exchanged a few words and then they got on their bikes and drove away. I asked my neighbour what he said and he told he said, "Don't piss off my neighbour or else there will be big trouble." My other neighbour came over later in the day when he heard what happened.

I told him the details and he asked if I got their badge numbers? I said no but I could describe them and my other neighbour can confirm it. I asked why he wanted to know this and he told me he was the Chief of the Malta police and these two officers were going to lose their jobs for treating me this way. He said no one yells at his neighbours. He said sometimes some cops get jealous of some peoples' cars and act with unacceptable behaviour to show they are tough. When they see resistance they get cocky and in my case when the neighbour came out they got scared and took off. So now I had the police on my side. But I did nothing wrong that day at all. Funny thing: My car had a banner across the windshield that said "Lost Angels" (was this sublimely trying to tell me something or was I just a target).

Our New Family

My wife became pregnant about a year after we got to Malta. We were both so happy with our new life in Malta and now we were going to start a family. I remember once during Arlette's pregnancy (she was about five months along) we were driving home and we were cut off. I lost it and was going after him, but Arlette freaked out and yelled at me in the car, "Are you psychotic?" The guy got out of his car, came to my door and began yelling at me. I hollered back, "You freaking moron. You cut me off and you're yelling at me?" He went back to his car and opened his trunk, I thought WTF! I thought he was getting a bat so I started to get out of my car because I was going to get him before he got me. He came towards me carrying a gas can and his lighter and asked me if I wanted a shower. I used to carry a knife in my car for camping so I reached to get it because I was going to stab this moron before he did anything. I was so angry that someone would threaten my life and my pregnant wife's and I wasn't going to have any of that.

Arlette slammed the glove compartment on my hand while still yelling at me. I told him I would be back tomorrow, by myself if he wanted to finish what he started and drove away. I returned every day but I ever did not see him again. What the hell was going on? Ahhh, life in Malta.

Arlette and I got a nice flat (apartment) near the water and we were expecting our first child. I remember taking photos of Arlette every month and remember how great she looked pregnant. She was and looked absolutely amazing through it all. We went for walks every day, drank cappuccino and just loved our life. We were especially looking forward to our upcoming new addition. We also loved our life because for the first time there were no problems or walls in front of us.

I remember Arlette telling me her sister's friend was coming for a visit with us and she needed me to pick her up at the airport.

We had planned that I would go to the airport, pick up her friend and the family would meet me there. When the flight landed and as the passengers came into the airport I remember seeing my brother-in-law standing with a video camera and all our family was there with him. It never even clued in. This lady and this little girl were coming down the stairs and I thought, "Wow, does she ever look like my Mom!" not thinking for a moment it was her. But it was her with my baby sister. What a surprise for me! This is why all the family was there and they had brought the video camera. It was so amazing having my Mom and sister come for a visit and knowing she would be with us for the birth of our first child. How exciting! Randy was born on November 28, 1995 at about two o'clock in the morning. I bet you are thinking that everything went smoothly, right?

Well—WRONG! There always seemed to be drama in my life and this special moment turned out to be no different. It did not go without a hitch.

I remember the Doctor was something else to be desired and I'm sure the midwives had been trained by him. I started raising my voice at one of them because Arlette was screaming she was in extreme pain and the midwife was merely telling her to just relax. I told her what I thought of her care (actually non-care) for Arlette and let her know in no uncertain terms that I was going to tell all of Malta what a bad midwife she was on the radio as I had contacts in the radio business. My father-in-law was the Managing Director of the radio station and the entertainment district, but more on that later. The Doctor and nurse kicked me out of the delivery room. Yes, they actually kicked me out, the father of the baby kicked out and I won't see my first child being born. WTF! So now Arlette was left on her own with who I felt were lunatics. I called her parents and my brother-in-law and was hysterical. I was so panicked, fearful for Arlette's well being and now here I was, kicked out and being kept away from her. What was I going to do? My in-laws and brother-in-law came running into the hospital and were concerned not only about Arlette, but about me as well because they thought I had lost my mind and was now so hopped up on coffee and cigarettes that I had become delusional.

Arlette finally gave birth to our son. I don't know what she really had to go through, but I do know she had multiple stitches and was in major pain. Randy was put into an incubator and they would not let me see him. I remember the Doctor coming out with the news that I was now the father of a healthy baby boy and everything went well. I was so happy and relieved that I almost collapsed. I remember the Doctor talking to my Father-in-law and I ran through the doors that were behind him so I could see my wife and our new son. I remember crying and saying how beautiful he was with his blue eyes and blonde hair, when in fact his eyes were brown and his hair was dark. Wow, that was some strong coffee I drank! I hugged Arlette, told her how much I loved her and then was escorted out of the hospital by security. Our first son was born and we were going to be set. I called my Mom and told her we had a boy. She was so happy and excited to be a grandmother for the first time. I remember she was booked to leave us the next day and we wanted her to stay a little longer so she could spend more time with her first grandchild. We had to pay a large sum just to keep her there the extra week but it was well worth it. We were now moving forward with our lives with our new baby.

Yee haw! Or so we thought.

I remember getting my papers from my employer advising me that they were laying off all the workers in my department along with a number of drivers, which meant I couldn't even stay on as a driver which I had been expecting to do. Were they kidding me? We had a new born child about a month and a half ago and this was happening. I didn't plan for this!

So, out went the resumes and shortly after I received a call for an interview with a major shipping line to run the operations at the terminal where the ships were located. Amazing. I had an interview with the big boys of Malta, but do you think I could get to it without issues? NOPE! See the pattern? I was excited about a new start and a new job opportunity. I remember it was shortly after Randy was born I think he was two months old. My wife and I were driving with Randy in his car seat in the back of the car. And guess what . . . cut off again! OH NO. YOU DIDN'T? YES I DID! I lost my mind, my temper escalated and away I went after him. I have a very bad temper and like a light switch it turned on. I chased his car and made him stop. I got out of the car in frenzy and went to him yelling, "Are you stupid? Didn't you see me?" He uttered something back and I told him I should beat the hell out of him right where he stood. I started to walk back to my car when I faintly heard Arlette yelling for me to look out. He blindsided me with a punch to the side of my head and eye area. At that point I totally lost my mind and proceeded to beat him to the ground. We were right in front of a police station and not even one person came out while this was going on. Arlette finally got out of the car and stopped the fight. We went on with the rest our day and by the time we got home I had a black eye and here I was with an interview scheduled for the next day. What was I going to do? I went to my interview the next day and there I sat with my eye swollen shut and black and blue. What a mess. My interview went well however but the boss kept looking at my eye and then I told him my nephew had hit me with a baseball. I got my nephew back for the ice cold water in the hot tub incident at my wedding by blaming this on him). He said, "Oh my God! Strong kid." I GOT THE JOB!! But the drama hadn't ended yet.

I started working the next day. My boss suggested we go downstairs for a beer and lunch which I agreed to. We walked into the cafeteria and lo and behold the guy I had fought with the day before my interview was right there in front of me, sitting in a corner with some other guy. We looked at each other. He had black eyes, a bandage on his nose (I think it was broken) and a badly cut up face and lip. I stood my ground as I thought he may be ready for round two, I knew I was. He got up and quickly left the room. My boss saw this subtle confrontation and looked puzzled. We sat down, ordered lunch and I told my boss I needed to talk to him about something I thought he should know. I proceeded to tell him about the fight I had with the guy who had just left and all he said in a broken English accent was to remind him not to 'piss' me off. He and I got along famously. We worked together for quite a while. I never saw that other guy ever again. Hmmmmm. I loved working in this area and was happy again.

We had great times in Malta and some not so great, but I loved every minute of it. I remember one weekend we decided to go to an island of Malta called Comino. (The movies 'Popeye' and 'Blue Lagoon' had parts filmed there.) We were having a great time and were watching people cliff jump. I was terrified of heights since my fall, so there was no way was I going near that sport.

I remember climbing up the cliff to watch the jumpers more closely. Two couples were getting ready to jump. One girl was particularly scared and the others were urging her to jump. "Jump! Jump! Jump!", they kept saying to her but she still refused and this annoyed her boyfriend. The other couple jumped while these two remained behind. I went in closer to see what they were going to do and then I saw him grab her and start to shove her towards the edge of the cliff. I didn't know whether he was only intending to joke with her or not, but down over the cliff she flew, landing on her back in the water. I nearly wet my pants. I couldn't believe what I had just witnessed. What kind of a guy does this? Now I wanted to push him off and see how he liked it. We saw that she had hit the water really hard and could see her begin fluttering like she couldn't get her breath at which time he began to panic. I also became concerned at what I was seeing. Not good! I know CPR and felt this was going to be a bad situation if I didn't do something quickly to help so off the cliff I jumped. Now I must mention that this jump was nearly an eighty foot drop. I think I counted to ten on my way down into the water. I tried to land near her, but not on her. I was successful. I grabbed her, put my arm around her neck, kept her on her back and swam her to shore where the others were now waiting. I remember my body was stinging from my landing in the water. I hated that jump, but I would do it again in a heartbeat. I would have just made sure to drop that boyfriend of hers over first. The girl was fine after a while, but I'm not sure what happened to them as a couple.

The rest of our trip was good, but Comino would come back to haunt me several times later.

We went away again with my sister-in-law and brother-in-law for a weekend of fun and drinking. I can remember being in a neck brace for some reason at that time and the Doctor telling me to "take it easy".

The four of us were having a great time together, drinking, swimming, horsing around and just enjoying each other's company. My brother-in-law and I were goofing around in the pool and then someone suggested we go windsurfing so off we went to do just that. We went to see the guy who rented the boards and he asked us if we had ever done this before. "OH YEAH, of course we have.", we said. Remember, I was in a neck brace. We got the boards and the sails and down to the water we went. There were only small gusts of wind which was not much to really sail with. I got up first then fell into the water. My brother-in-law was up on his board and he started to move out. I finally got up again but those things are heavy and with a neck brace on, they were even heavier. Just as I got up a gust of wind came and sent me flying along the water. I slammed right into the side of a large boat and down I went again. Now I was sore and in the water again. I remember my brother-in-law going down a few more times as well. I did get it going again and this time I really started to travel a distance from the shore. I fell again and decided to just sit on the board for a little while because I was exhausted and I wanted to rest my neck for a while too. I had been sitting there for about five minutes when I remember hearing chatter over where my wife was sitting for sun tanning and then I saw her near the water's edge and she jumped into the water. I thought she was swimming and she started to head out towards me as people on the shore were urging her on. I was puzzled and was wondering what was going on. I could hear her yelling, "I'm coming, Honey." I thought, "Coming where?" I was relaxing and yet it seemed like she was coming to save me. I kept telling her not to come out, but she never listened. She does that from time to time. She swam all the way out to me, climbed on the board and I said, "Now what?" She signalled for a guy to come get us so the guy gets in a boat and heads out towards us and I'm shaking my head because I don't know what is going on. We get towed to shore and I remember the people standing on the cliff edge by the hotel cheering for Arlette because 'she had just saved my life'. I was never in any trouble. I had just decided to sit, relax, and enjoy the scenery while I rested. It was so funny. She always tells the story of the day she saved my life. (She has done it a thousand times since then.)

After that we went cliff jumping (only twenty feet high this time). What a great weekend, but did it do a number on my neck.

We had made several trips to Comino and it seemed something crazy always happened to me while we were there. Cliff jumping to rescue someone, wind surfing only to be 'rescued', and so much more. I can remember how bad my sister-in-law was when she was on the boats going back and forth. She was never good with the motion of the sea so there is always a story to be told about that.

I remember how snorkelling was always amazing to me and I was lucky enough to enjoy it several times while I lived in Malta. Seeing the crystal clear water like that was an awesome experience and not done by too many people. I saw incredible fish, squid, and even eels. I saw rock formations and caves that just had to be explored and explore them we did. I remember one very long cave that had a couple of areas where we could come up for air and plan our next stage like we were scuba diving to the Titanic. I recall one time my brother-in-law and I were going through a cave and had agreed that if either of us encountered anything we would kind of garble through our snorkels to each other so we would be aware. I remember getting ahead of my brother-in-law and exploring every nook and cranny. Suddenly I was stung by a huge jelly fish or maybe it was a bunch of them and was it painful. I screamed through my snorkel, "OUCH! OUCH! OUCH!" and I guess it sounded like "SHARK" because my brother-in-law bolted right out of that water and I swear I saw the wake gathering behind him like he was a speed boat he moved so fast. I made my way out too but the pain was intense. I didn't know what to do about it. We tried washing my bright red body with the salt water, but to no avail. It was useless. I swear I was in pain for hours. I would later learn that for whatever reason urinating on it would have helped. Had I known that, you could have used me as a toilet and I would not have cared in the least. I would have even begged you to do it. Whatever it takes!

There were also the many trips we made to the island of Gozo, which is another Malta island. We would take the ferry across from Malta with our car so we would be able to drive around everywhere. We would spend weekends there as a mini vacation away from home and we would go there for special occasions as well. My in-laws would rent a flat (apartment) with a pool for the family and we would all go there together. We had so much fun. We would have a place with a pool and then we would have the sea fifty feet away. They had beautiful restaurants there that would be magical to eat at, with the exception of the one time we were there with our son when he was about a year old. We ordered a seafood platter and drinks but our little one screamed so much that when our dinner came we had to leave it there and go back to our apartment. Nothing was wrong with him. He just wanted to vent I guess. Cost me nearly a Hundred Dollars as a result of that tirade. I should bill him for it. We spent many family days there and visited their numerous beautiful churches and monuments. They were all just beautiful sites and honestly I could not get enough of the pure history of the place. I always hated history class but I loved the history of Gozo.

Oh, those gorgeous sunsets and the romantic dinners, the beautiful homes and sights. I'm getting home sick just thinking about it and remembering all those wonderful times.

We saw a Ziggy Marley concert on the beach and had a meet and greet with him. What an awesome experience that was. Imagine a sunset concert on a beautiful beach, fabulous music, dancing until sunrise and beer, beer, beer and more beer. We even saw The Mad Stuntman (he sang the song 'I LIKE TO MOVE IT, MOVE IT)'. We went to the hotel where he was staying. He had a special cane he used in his videos as a prop and he gave it to my nephew (Ahhh yes. Good times and memories).

I loved Malta, but my wife's feelings for our new home were starting to change toward it. She began to miss Canada. (Why that was I could never figure out.)

My sister-in-law and brother-in-law left Malta in 1997 and returned to Canada. It was from this point that my wife started asking me if we could return. I reluctantly agreed and we started the planning for our return to Canada. We had spent five years in Malta and I loved every minute of it. We had our first child, great jobs, a house, a car, health, happiness. What more could we want than that?

Well there is one thing . . . if I could change one thing that happened in Malta, it would be the falling out I had with my sister-in-law and my brother-in-law. That falling out cost me the relationship I had with them and I don't know if we will ever get it back. Things have never been the same between us since then but I do know I would give anything to make this right between us and to tell them I am sorry. They will never know how much I miss them, the closeness and friendship we had, and the times we spent together. I lost something very valuable and meaningful, I know. I would really want to change that.

Return To Canada

e returned to Canada in 1998 for another beginning and although everything seemed like it would be fine, we had unseen problems coming our way in the future. **BIG TIME**

One bonus with our return was that I quit drinking and smoking. I think my body just had too much and I knew it was time to stop.

We both had secured very good employment. I started with a company in Toronto whose partner company had been headhunting me in Malta to work for them. We bought a car and we were settling in the city quite well. We stayed with relatives at the beginning, eventually rented our own place for a while and then in December, 1998 we purchased our own house. We eagerly moved in and we loved it. We settled down, again, and began planning our family's future and for our new life back in Canada. The only setback we had then was the death of my Aunt and then my Grandmother in late 1998. It was a devastating time for Arlette and me as the deaths happened so close together and we were both exceptionally close with my Grandmother. But I'm glad we were back in Canada when it happened and were able to say our goodbyes. As time moved forward we were happy, loving life and our second beautiful child, Jason, was born in November, 1999.

I had started playing hockey again and remember moving up the ranks very fast. I had made the All Star team several times and won numerous championships. I had even travelled in Ontario for tournaments and was having a great time doing so. I also loved golf and golfed many times in tournaments as well, with my work, my friends and with my brother and Dad.

I remember this one time when my Dad, myself, my sister's ex-husband and Don went to play golf together and we were having a great time bonding. We had to go to this hole that was down a huge hill and had a ninety degree left turn to the tee. I remember I was driving the golf cart with only Don and me in it. We headed down this hill to the aforementioned hole and the golf cart was picking up quite a bit of speed. I decided not to hit the brake because I wanted to see just how fast I could get the golf cart to go. As we got to the bottom of the hill I turned the steering wheel hard left, which caused us to skid and over we went—right up on two wheels. Don fell right out of the golf cart and our clubs went flying. He lost it. He was so scared and he was yelling that I was crazy and he was not driving with me again. It was so funny! Then I looked around and realized it could have ended so much worse. Not funny! There was a narrow line of bushes that we had finally stopped right beside which I saw was covering the huge cliffside to the lower tees where we were heading in the cart. Had we not stopped when we did, we could have gone over the cliff and may have surely been killed, or at the least maimed. I drove the rest of the course by myself as no one would drive with me and I couldn't blame them. Definitely not funny! (Actually, in looking back, it was!!)

I still had fun bumping the cart that they were all crammed into and doing donuts and skids all over the course. We still talk about this all the time and laugh so hard. I wonder how Don would feel if I asked him about this now? I remember golfing many times and always having an adventure in this sport—so to speak.

I remember my in-laws were coming for a visit in 2000. I believe I had a hockey game scheduled on the night they were going to arrive. The lexan visor for my goalie helmet was bothering me as it kept fogging up (the visor hangs from my helmet to protect my neck) so I removed it on the bench just before my game. **Big Mistake.** I guess you can see where this is heading?

I remember a player coming in very close and taking the big slap shot (I guess he was at the hash marks which is the two lines on the big circle close to the goalie nets). The puck hit me right in the throat and down I went. I could hardly breathe and thought I was going to die right then and there it was so painful. I was rushed home with most of my equipment still on and we went to straight to the hospital. My vocal cords and larynx had been crushed from the impact of that shot to the throat. I was on a liquid diet for three weeks, Boost, milk shakes, and anything else we could put in the blender. I remember writing words on cards for my Mother-in-law and her laughing and saying how quiet it was now. It was one of the most painful hockey injuries I have ever received in all the years playing that game. But it wasn't going to be the last of the pain I would endure. I went back to playing hockey a few weeks or so later against Doctors' orders and never wore my throat guard again. How strange is that?

I broke some records and had some great years following that incident, but again it would all come crashing down on me.

I remember while playing hockey, even sometimes in normal everyday life, having some issues with my vision and various odd feelings throughout my body, but we always attributed it to one of my car accidents or one of the many injuries I had sustained during my lifetime. I always played sports and was very active doing many things, so no thought of a disease, much less Multiple Sclerosis, was ever on my mind. I have a cousin who has MS. He was diagnosed many years ago, I believe in 1988. He lives out west and we don't talk, but I never imagined or ever gave it a moment's thought it would happen to me. I was always active, pretty healthy and very naïve. I just didn't know any better. I recall a time when I lost the vision in my left eye completely for a few days and was terrified I might be going blind. I went to the Doctor, had drops put in my eyes and waited for a few more days but nothing changed, so we booked an appointment to see an eye doctor. By the time my appointment arrived my vision had returned so I didn't go to see him. Didn't feel the need too since it was better. This happened on a smaller scale a few more times after that but we always said it would come back again soon so for me to just have patience. I continued on with my life as I always did.

THE TWO WORST LETTERS
I WOULD EVER HEAR

M&S

I was playing hockey on a Thursday night. I remember it so well. I took a slap shot to the chest. (I was a goalie as you may remember.) I knew the puck caused some damage as soon as it struck me. I was suddenly in severe pain and even had trouble breathing. I knew my ribs were broken again, but I continued to play in this condition until the end of the game. By the time we got to the dressing room I saw my chest was black and blue and it was extremely sore. The next day I went to have it looked at and the Doctor confirmed I did indeed have broken ribs—again! He told me I would need four to six weeks to heal from the injury. I told him I had a game in four days to which he informed me I wouldn't be playing. I thought about what I might be able to do so I could play in my condition. Then I had an idea . . . a dumb one, but an idea. I taped a throw pillow from our couch to my chest and off I went to play in that Tuesday night game, all the while thinking—awh, it couldn't happen again. I played into the second period and then the unthinkable happened. I made a save and a guy fell on top of me. Snap!! I screamed. I knew instantly I was in trouble. I immediately stopped playing this time. I went home in so much pain and in the morning I paid the Doctor another visit. Needless to say he was not the least bit impressed. I had broken another rib so now I had four broken ribs and again on the same side as my work accident injury in Malta. I took time away from hockey in order to heal and while I was doing this I started to notice some strange tingling in my hands, feet and neck. My neck had always had the tingles since my car accident but this time it seemed worse.

I went back to the Doctor's a couple of weeks later to see what causing this tingling sensation as it was driving me crazy. He asked a series of in-depth questions and then he did some blood work on me. About a week later he called me to come into his office so I stopped in to see him on my way to work.

I remember so vividly him telling me to sit down because we needed to talk. I thought he was going to give me a strong lecture for playing hockey too soon after the injury.

He asked me if I ever heard of MS? Oh boy, I thought to myself, "Now how long does this mean I will have to miss hockey?" At this time it never dawned on me about my cousin having MS because it was only mentioned to me that he had it, not what is was and as I said, I had never given any thought to it. I figured MS had something to do with the ribs and it was going to delay me getting back into the net which did not make me happy. He explained what MS was EXACTLY to me and I sat listening, STUNNED! I was so scared, no—I was literally terrified. And then he said these words to me in this one sentence that would change my life forever:

"I think you have MS."

I remember telling him I didn't have time for MS. I have hockey. I didn't even know what MS was. Here I was thinking my symptom was something to do with my rib injury. I was devastated by this news and remember coming home, telling Arlette and crying uncontrollably because, after what I had just learned about this disease, I thought I was going to die from it. I remember going back to work later that morning and telling my boss my news. He hugged me as he said, "OH MY GOD!" He told me that his Mom had died a number of years ago and that she had MS. Then I really lost it again, my jaw dropped to the floor. I thought

I had just been a handed a death sentence that morning by the Doctor, and here I went to work only to learn firsthand that someone actually did die from it. They sat me down and talked to me while another colleague contacted Arlette to see how she was doing. She was freaking out and was calling everyone she could to tell them this terrible news. My employer told me to go home and take as much time as I needed to sort things out. I remember calling the Doctor and telling him I wanted a second opinion. He suggested we do an MRI (Magnetic Resonance Imaging). I did one the following week and the results came back positive. I didn't believe it so I requested another MRI. Results came back positive from the second one as well. So On October 31, 2002 (Halloween) I, Mark Stewart, was officially confirmed and diagnosed with Multiple Sclerosis. I took a week off work so I could study what MS was and find what I could do to fight it. I said, "I have MS, MS doesn't have me.", but would I be proven wrong later. What is MS? Well it stands for Multiple Sclerosis. The technical definition is as follows:

What exactly is Multiple Sclerosis? I have been asked this question many times. I have always tried to explain it in easy terms for all to understand.

I always say think of a computer, the keyboard (your spinal cord) and monitor (your brain). If you push the letter **M**, then **M** comes up on the screen. Push an **S** and same thing, an **S** appears. Then think if you were to put a small cut into the squiggly wire that attaches the keyboard to the computer and push a letter again, it may not come up or it may take a minute to work. If you were to put several nicks into that wire you may get different signals. These are what we call Sclerosis and when you have many different signals it is Multiple Sclerosis. It is multiple scars on the brain and spinal cord. This is kind of how our brain works with Multiple Sclerosis. We are trying to do things like we always did but we are not getting the signal to react correctly. My mind says walk and my body says don't move, or cramp up, or go into violent convulsions.

Side note: The one truly positive thing that came from my diagnosis was the birth of our third child Dylan in December, 2006. We were told that I wouldn't be able to have any more children and then along came this little miracle. We were not planning for another addition to our family so needless to say it was a big surprise for us and it turned out to be an amazing one. He is, and always has been a fire cracker with energy to burn. We all laugh every day at the way he behaves and the outrageous things he says. He is really into hockey and reminds me so much of myself. He will definitely grow to be a great man like his amazing brothers. I am so very proud of each of my sons and I know they will make great husbands and fathers when they to start their families.

We decided we had better put a stop to the baby making process (the factory, not the job itself). And it was decided that I would get 'fixed'. I guess that was a bet I lost big time. Remember how afraid of needles I am? Well, can you guess what else I did with no freezing? Yep! That too. Arlette said she heard me screaming all the way down the hall in the hospital. Even the Doctor was amazed. What was I thinking? We didn't have frozen vegetables for weeks . . . my recovery strategy!

Our Wedding & Limo

Mark & Arlette
enjoying lunch

after CCSVI surgery
holding Dylan

Back Row Randy, Jason, Arlette

Malta Feast= Party time

Mark in wheelchair

What were they thinking 8 years old

Malta sunrise. This is life

Rick Hansen relay
Many in Motion 2011

TEN QUESTIONS OF MS

If I was to be asked what would be the top ten questions regarding MS that I am asked or I would hear I would probably say the following:

1. What is Multiple Sclerosis?
2. Is there a cure?
3. Does Multiple Sclerosis kill you?
4. How did you get it?
5. Is it in your genes/hereditary?
6. How did your family react?
7. What are you going to do?
8. Is it contagious?
9. Why?
10. Who gets Multiple Sclerosis?

Answers I can give:

1. Multiple Sclerosis is a chronic and often disabling disease of the central nervous system. In young adults, it is one of the most common central nervous system diseases.

    Sclerosis are "scars" such as plaques or lesions in the brain and spinal cord. Multiple Sclerosis is a progressive disease in which scattered patches of the protective myelin sheath covering of the nerve fibers in the brain and spine (the central nervous system) are damaged or destroyed.

    Myelin is a fatty material around nerves that acts like the insulation around electrical wires. When the myelin sheath is damaged, the electrical impulses along the nerves are disrupted. This disruption affects many functions of the body.

    Symptoms may be mild (e.g., numbness in the limbs) or severe (e.g., paralysis or loss of vision).

    The progress, severity and specific symptoms of Multiple Sclerosis in any one person cannot yet be predicted, but advances in research and treatment are giving hope to those affected by the disease.

2. There are no drugs or treatment protocols that can cure Multiple Sclerosis. There are currently treatments which can modify the course of the disease. However, research is ongoing to find both effective means of preventing and arresting the disease, as well as developing better ways of treating those who have Multiple Sclerosis. In recent years there have been advances on many fronts. Treatments have been developed that reduce the number and severity of relapses in some people with Multiple Sclerosis. In addition, there are therapies to relieve many symptoms and improve the quality of life of people with Multiple Sclerosis.

3. No. Multiple Sclerosis is not a fatal disease and individuals can be expected to have normal or near normal life expectancy. In fact, the majority of people with Multiple Sclerosis do not become severely disabled. Two-thirds of people with Multiple Sclerosis are able to walk with or without the use of aides and continue to lead productive and satisfying lives.

4. Not totally sure. But this book may explain what may have brought it out.

5. Studies indicate that genetic factors *may* make certain individuals more susceptible to the disease, but there is no evidence that Multiple Sclerosis is directly inherited.

6. Very hard and yet very supportive. My wife has taken on a whole new proverbial child who will never grow up to walk and run again and the loss of a husband has been hard but she is amazing. I think this book explains just how strong you have to become after being diagnosed with any illness to be able to cope with it.

7. Not sure yet. I fight this illness every day and every day I feel something different. Anger, frustration, hatred, misery, pain, depression are all feelings I have regularly but I have a family I need to fight for and I will do it for them.

8. No . . . Multiple Sclerosis is not contagious. So kiss us. It's okay.

9. Just not sure. But I will ask God when I get there.

10. Multiple Sclerosis affects women 50% more than men or, if you prefer ratios, 3 to 2. Most people with Multiple Sclerosis are diagnosed between the ages

of 20 and 40. Multiple Sclerosis is rarely found in people younger than 12 or older than 55. Multiple Sclerosis is more common among Caucasians than other races. This is particularly true with those of Northern European ancestry. In some populations, such as Eskimos, Multiple Sclerosis is practically unheard of. Multiple Sclerosis is more common farther from the equator. Some studies have reported that Multiple Sclerosis is as much as five times more likely in North America and Europe than in the tropics.

Multiple Sclerosis is defined as:

MS; Demyelinising Disease

Multiple sclerosis (abbreviated MS, known as *disseminated sclerosis* or *encephalomyelitis disseminata*) is an inflammatory disease in which the fatty myelin sheaths around the axons of the brain and spinal cord are damaged, leading to demyelination and scarring as well as a broad spectrum of signs and symptoms. Disease onset usually occurs in young adults, and it is more common in women. It has a prevalence that ranges between 2 and 150 per 100,000. MS was first described in 1868 by Jean-Martin Charcot.

Side note: MS affects the ability of nerve cells in the brain and spinal cord to communicate with each other effectively. Nerve cells communicate by sending electrical signals called <u>action potentials</u> down long fibers called <u>axons</u>, which are contained within an insulating substance called <u>myelin</u>. In MS, the body's own <u>immune system</u> attacks and damages the myelin. When myelin is lost, the axons can no longer effectively conduct signals. The name *multiple sclerosis* refers to scars (scleroses—better known as plaques or lesions) particularly in the <u>white matter</u> of the brain and spinal cord, which is mainly composed of myelin. Although much is known about the mechanisms involved in the disease process, the cause remains unknown. Theories include <u>genetics</u> or <u>infections</u>. Different environmental <u>risk factors</u> have also been found.

Almost any neurological <u>symptom</u> can appear with the disease, and often progresses to physical and <u>cognitive disability</u>. MS takes several forms, with new symptoms occurring either in discrete attacks (relapsing forms) or slowly accumulating over time (progressive forms) Between attacks, symptoms may go away completely, but permanent neurological problems often occur, especially as the disease advances.

There is no known cure for multiple sclerosis. Treatments attempt to return function after an attack, prevent new attacks, and prevent disability. MS medications can have adverse effects or be poorly tolerated, and many patients pursue alternative treatments, despite the lack of supporting scientific study. The <u>prognosis</u> is difficult to predict; it depends on the subtype of the disease, the individual patient's disease characteristics, the initial symptoms and the degree of disability the person experiences as time advances. <u>Life expectancy</u> of people with MS is 5 to 10 years lower than that of the unaffected population.

Several subtypes, or patterns of progression, have been described. Subtypes use the past course of the disease in an attempt to <u>predict</u> the future course. They are important not only for prognosis but also for therapeutic decisions. In 1996 the United States <u>National Multiple Sclerosis Society</u> standardized four subtype definitions:

1. relapsing remitting,
2. secondary progressive,
3. primary progressive, and
4. progressive relapsing.

Side note: I was diagnosed with primary progressive MS on October 31 of 2001

The **relapsing-remitting** subtype is characterized by unpredictable relapses followed by periods of months to years of relative quiet (remission) with no new signs of disease activity. Deficits suffered during attacks may either resolve or leave sequelae, the latter being more common as a function of time. This describes the initial course of 80% of individuals with MS. When deficits always resolve between attacks, this is sometimes referred to as benign MS, although patients will still accrue some degree of disability in the long term. The relapsing-remitting subtype usually begins with a clinically isolated syndrome (CIS). In CIS, a patient has an attack suggestive of demyelination, but does not fulfill the criteria for multiple sclerosis. However only 30 to 70% of persons experiencing CIS later develop MS.

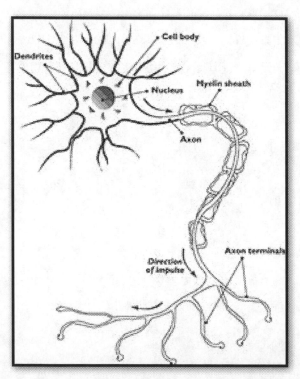

Nerve axon with myelin sheath

Secondary progressive MS (sometimes called "galloping MS") describes around 65% of those with an initial relapsing-remitting MS, who then begin to have progressive neurologic decline between acute attacks without any definite periods of remission. Occasional relapses and minor remissions may appear. The median time between disease onset and conversion from relapsing-remitting to secondary progressive MS is 19 years.

Primary progressive subtype describes the approximately 10–15% of individuals who never have remission after their initial MS symptoms. It is characterized by progression of disability from onset, with no, or only occasional and minor, remissions and improvements.

The age of onset for the **primary progressive** subtype is later than for the relapsing-remitting, but similar to mean age of progression between the relapsing-remitting and the secondary progressive. In both cases it is around 40 years of age.

Progressive relapsing MS describes those individuals who, from onset, have a steady neurologic decline but also suffer clear superimposed attacks. This is the least common of all subtypes.

Atypical variants of MS with non-standard behavior have been described; these include Devic's disease, Balo concentric sclerosis, Schilder's diffuse sclerosis and Marburg multiple sclerosis. There is debate on whether they are MS variants or different diseases. Multiple sclerosis also behaves differently in children, taking more time to reach the progressive stage. Nevertheless they still reach it at a lower mean age than adults.

Causes, incidence, and risk factors

Multiple sclerosis (MS) affects women more than men. The disorder is most commonly diagnosed between ages 20 and 40, but can be seen at any age.

MS is caused by damage to the myelin sheath, the protective covering that surrounds nerve cells. When this nerve covering is damaged, nerve impulses are slowed down or stopped.

The nerve damage is caused by inflammation. Inflammation occurs when the body's own immune cells attack the nervous system. Repeated episodes of inflammation can occur along any area of the brain, optic nerve, and spinal cord.

Researchers are not sure what triggers the inflammation. The most common theories point to a virus or genetic defect, or a combination of both. Geographic studies indicate there may be an environmental factor involved.

People with a family history of MS and those who live in a geographical area where MS is more common have a slightly higher risk of the disease.

Symptoms

Symptoms vary, because the location and severity of each attack can be different. Episodes can last for days, weeks, or months. These episodes alternate with periods of reduced or no symptoms (remissions).

Fever, hot baths, sun exposure, and stress can trigger or worsen attacks.

It is common for the disease to return (relapse). However, the disease may continue to get worse without periods of remission.

Because nerves in any part of the brain or spinal cord may be damaged, patients with multiple sclerosis can have symptoms in many parts of the body.

Muscle symptoms:

- Loss of balance
- Muscle spasms
- Numbness or abnormal sensation in any area
- Problems moving arms or legs
- Problems walking
- Problems with coordination and making small movements
- Tremor in one or more arms or legs
- Weakness in one or more arms or legs

Bowel and bladder symptoms:

- Constipation and stool leakage
- Difficulty beginning to urinate
- Frequent need to urinate
- Strong urge to urinate
- Urine leakage (incontinence)

Eye symptoms:

- Double vision
- Eye discomfort
- Uncontrollable rapid eye movements
- Vision loss (usually affects one eye at a time)

Numbness, tingling, or pain

- Facial pain
- Painful muscle spasms
- Tingling, crawling, or burning feeling in the arms and legs

Other brain and nerve symptoms:

- Decreased attention span, poor judgment, and memory loss
- Difficulty reasoning and solving problems
- Depression or feelings of sadness
- Dizziness and balance problems
- Hearing loss

Sexual symptoms:

- Problems with erections
- Problems with vaginal lubrication

Speech and swallowing symptoms:

- Slurred or difficult-to-understand speech
- Trouble chewing and swallowing

Fatigue is a common and bothersome symptoms as MS progresses. It is often worse in the late afternoon.

Signs and tests:

Symptoms of MS may mimic those of many other nervous system disorders. The disease is diagnosed by ruling out other conditions.

People who have a form of MS called relapsing-remitting may have a history of at least two attacks, separated by a period of reduced or no symptoms.

The health care provider may suspect MS if there are decreases in the function of two different parts of the central nervous system (such as abnormal reflexes) at two different times.

A neurological exam may show reduced nerve function in one area of the body, or spread over many parts of the body. This may include:

- Abnormal nerve reflexes
- Decreased ability to move a part of the body
- Decreased or abnormal sensation
- Other loss of nervous system functions

An eye examination may show:

- Abnormal pupil responses
- Changes in the visual fields or eye movements
- Decreased visual acuity
- Problems with the inside parts of the eye
- Rapid eye movements triggered when the eye moves

Tests to diagnose multiple sclerosis include:

- Lumbar puncture (spinal tap) for cerebrospinal fluid tests, including CSF oligoclonal banding
- MRI scan of the brain and MRI scan of the spine are important to help diagnose and follow MS
- Nerve function study (evoked potential test)

My Doctor recommended a neurologist and I went to see her. She seemed more interested in my health card than my health. I remember her saying, "Health card." before she said, "Hi Mark." She would spend five minutes with me and say, "Okay. Come back in two weeks and we'll do the next test." I wondered what the hell she was doing, Then, on the next visit, "Health card please." again. The last time I saw her I told her, "I will give you my health card when I'm satisfied you did something to earn it." So she jabbed me with a series of needles and said she was reading an electric gram or something (evoked potential test). I remember telling her she was doing nothing for me and moving on to someone else.

I had all of the above tests and must say they all left a lot to be desired for me.

I started to see a new neurologist and I was happy. He seemed more knowledgeable (at least in my mind he was) although he seemed to be always leaning towards drugs for me. I was prescribed *drugs such as:

(*Here I'm going to give the name and description of the drugs. You do not have to read it but it is informative for those who would like to know the details.)

Morphine: *one of at least 50 alkaloids of several different types present in opium, Poppy Straw Concentrate, and other poppy derivatives. Morphine is generally 8 to 17 percent of the dry weight of opium, although specially-bred cultivars reach 26 percent or produce little morphine at all, under 1 percent, perhaps down to 0.04 percent. The latter varieties, including the 'Przemko' and 'Norman' cultivars of the opium poppy, are used to produce two other alkaloids, thebaine and oripavine, which are used in the manufacture of semi-synthetic and synthetic opioids like oxycodone and etorphine and some other types of drugs. P. bracteatum does not contain morphine or codeine, or other narcotic phenanthrene-type, alkaloids. This species* is *rather a source* of thebaine. Occurrence of morphine in other papaverales and papaveraceae, as well as in some species of hops and mulberry trees has not been confirmed. Morphine is produced most predominantly early in the life cycle of the plant. Past the optimum point for extraction, various processes in the plant produce codeine, thebaine, and in some cases negligible amounts of hydromorphone, dihydromorphine, dihydrocodeine, tetrahydrothebaine, and hydrocodone (these compounds are rather synthesized from thebaine and oripavine). The human body produces endorphines, which are neuropeptides, with similar effects. In cli(MS Contin, MSIR, Avinza, Kadian, Oramorph, Roxanol, Kapanol) is a potent opiate analgesic medication and is considered to be the prototypical opioid. It was first isolated in 1804 by Friedrich Sertürner, first distributed by same in 1817, and first commercially sold by Merck in 1827, which at the time was a single small chemists' shop. It was more widely used after the invention of the hypodermic needle in 1857. It took its name from the Greek god of dreams Morpheus Morphine is the most abundant alkaloid found in opium, the dried sap (latex) derived from shallowly slicing the unripe seedpods of the opium, or common and/ or edible, poppy, Papaver somniferum. Morphine was the first active principle purified from a plant source and is nical medicine, morphine is regarded as the gold standard, or benchmark, of analgesics used to relieve severe or agonizing pain and suffering. Like other opioids, such as oxycodone,

157

hydromorphone, and diacetylmorphine (heroin), morphine acts directly on the central nervous system (CNS) to relieve pain. Unlike many other opioids, morphine is an opiate and a natural product. Morphine has a high potential for addiction; tolerance and psychological dependence develop rapidly, although physiological dependence may take several months to develop.)

Oxy-cotton: (**Oxycodone** is an opioid analgesic medication synthesized from opium-derived thebaine. It was developed in 1916 in Germany[5][6], as one of several new semi-synthetic opioids in an attempt to improve on the existing opioids: morphine, diacetylmorphine (heroin), and codeine[1] Oxycodone oral medications are generally prescribed for the relief of moderate to severe pain. Currently it is formulated as single ingredient products or compounded products. Some common examples of compounding are oxycodone with acetaminophen/paracetamol or NSAIDs such as ibuprofen. The formulations are available as generics but are also made under various brand names. OxyContin is Purdue Pharma's brand for time-release oral. oxycodone. The manufacturing rights to time-released generic oxycodone are under dispute.

Vicodin: **Hydrocodone** or **dihydrocodeinone** is a semi-synthetic opioid derived from either of two naturally occurring opiates: codeine[1] and thebaine[2]. It is an orally active <u>narcotic</u> <u>analgesic</u> (pain reliever) and <u>antitussive</u> (cough suppressant). It is commonly available in tablet, capsule, and syrup form, and is often compounded with other, generally less effective non-opioid compounds such as <u>paracetamol</u> (also known as acetaminophen) or <u>ibuprofen</u>, both often added to discourage recreational use[citation needed] (as paracetamol can cause potentially fatal liver toxicity at high doses), and to provide a possible synergy of analgesic effects between hydrocodone and the non-opioid compounds present. The particular niche in which hydrocodone is most commonly used is as an intermediate centrally acting analgesic. Abrupt discontinuation of hydrocodone (Vicodin, Vicodin ES, and Norco) may result in withdrawal symptoms.

Tylenol 3's and anything else for the pain and what was to come. Every medication had a side effect and there was always another drug for the side effect of the previous drug, so a vicious circle of drugs and drips were set up for me.

> When we first saw the new neurologist we were so naïve so we didn't really question anything as we just didn't know any better. He prescribed for me a medication called Betaseron, He felt that this would be the best medication for my MS, but didn't let me know of possible allergic reactions to it. He

did mention some side effects but nothing else. It however seems that a percentage of people may have allergic reactions to this and I was one of them. Mine was unfortunately far more severe.

Side note: It is very important you find a neurologist that you can trust completely with your health and decisions and to be an advocate for <u>you </u>in all aspects of your treatment. You know your body and you must trust yourself. Be informed and be educated and ask questions even if they seem irrelevant.

The simple side effects are listed here:

- **Side Effects:** The side effects of Betaseron are similar to those of other interferon-based therapies with the exception of Avonex, which doesn't cause as many injection-site reactions.

- **Flu-like Symptoms:** The most important side effect is the flu-like symptoms, which are experienced by about 76% of patients. These include fever, chills, sweating, muscle aches and fatigue, which last for 24 to 36 hours. This side effect is usually the worst after the first injection and progressively lessens with each injection, so that most people do experience it or it is tolerable after six months. It can also be reduced by starting with a low dose and increasing to a full dose gradually, over several weeks. Taking ibuprofen or acetaminophen a couple hours before and after can help with some of these side effects.

- **Red spots**: These usually occur at the site of injections (in 85% of patients), which may last several weeks. These can break down into sores (injection-site necrosis) in 4% of cases.

- **Liver Damage:** Hepatic injury including elevated serum hepatic enzyme levels and hepatitis has been reported. Regular monitoring is required to prevent such damage from occurring or progressing.

- **Blood Counts:** Betaseron can cause a decrease in the numbers of red and white blood cells, as well as a reduction in the number of platelets in the blood.
- **Depression:** Betaseron should be used with caution in patients with depression.

Something very important that also was not told to us:

Anaphylaxis and Allergic Reactions

Anaphylaxis has been reported as a rare complication of Betaseron ® use.

Other allergic reactions attributed to the use of Betaseron ® have included dyspnea (difficulty breathing), bronchospasm, tongue edema (swollen tongue), skin rash and urticaria (hives).

Some patients taking Betaseron have had severe allergic reactions leading to difficulty breathing and swallowing; these reactions can happen quickly.

Allergic reactions can happen after your first dose or may not happen until after you have taken Betaseron many times.

Less severe allergic reactions such as rash, itching, skin bumps or swelling of the mouth and tongue can also happen.

If you think you are having an allergic reaction, stop using Betaseron immediately and call your doctor.

Side note: We, as Multiple Sclerosis patients, need to be informed fully of all possible side effects of all medications we are prescribed or possibly thinking of starting. Educate yourself fully on all medications before starting.

*More on my allergic reactions further down, but I want to share possible treatments available

There are many possible treatments for Multiple Sclerosis to help slow the progression:

Treatment

There is no known cure for multiple sclerosis at this time. However, there are therapies that may slow the disease. The goal of treatment is to control symptoms and help you maintain a normal quality of life.

Medications used to slow the progression of multiple sclerosis are taken on a long-term basis, they include:

- Interferons (Avonex, Betaseron, or Rebif), glatiramer acetate (Copaxone), mitoxantrone (Novantrone), and natalizumab (Tysabri)
- Fingolimod (Gilenya)
- Methotrexate, azathioprine (Imuran), intravenous immunoglobulin (IVIg) and cyclophosphamide (Cytoxan) may also be used if the above drugs are not working well

Steroids may be used to decrease the severity of attacks.

Medications to control symptoms may include:

- Medicines to reduce muscle spasms such as Lioresal (Baclofen), tizanidine (Zanaflex), or a benzodiazepine
- Cholinergic medications to reduce urinary problems
- Antidepressants for mood or behavior symptoms
- Amantadine for fatigue

For more information see:

- Neurogenic bladder
- Bowel retraining

The following may also be helpful for people with MS:

- Physical therapy, speech therapy, occupational therapy, and support groups
- Assistive devices, such as wheelchairs, bed lifts, shower chairs, walkers, and wall bars
- A planned exercise program early in the course of the disorder
- A healthy lifestyle, with good nutrition and enough rest and relaxation

- Avoiding fatigue, stress, temperature extremes, and illness
- Changes in what you eat or drink if there are swallowing problems
- Making changes around the home to prevent falls

Household changes to ensure safety and ease in moving around the home are often needed.

> *I wish they had told me of the side effects of the medication I was prescribed as I wound up with Ulcerative Colitis and a very bad case of it.

Ulcerative colitis (Colitis ulcerosa, UC) is a form of inflammatory bowel disease (IBD). Ulcerative colitis is a form of colitis, a disease of the intestine, specifically the large intestine or colon, that includes characteristic ulcers, or open sores, in the colon. The main symptom of active disease is usually constant diarrhea mixed with blood, of gradual onset. IBD is often confused with irritable bowel syndrome (IBS), a troublesome, but much less serious, condition. Ulcerative colitis has similarities to Crohn's disease, another form of IBD. Ulcerative colitis is an intermittent disease, with periods of exacerbated symptoms, and periods that are relatively symptom-free. Although the symptoms of ulcerative colitis can sometimes diminish on their own the disease usually requires treatment to go into remission.

Ulcerative colitis occurs in 35–100 people for every 100,000 in the United States or less than 0.1% of the population. The disease is more prevalent in northern countries of the world, as well as in northern areas of individual countries or other regions. Although ulcerative colitis has no known cause, there is a presumed genetic component to susceptibility. The disease may be triggered in a susceptible person by environmental factors. Although dietary modification may reduce the discomfort of a person with the disease, ulcerative colitis is not thought to be caused by dietary factors. Although ulcerative colitis is treated as though it were an autoimmune disease, there is no consensus that it is such. Treatment is with anti-inflammatory drugs, immunosuppressant, and biological therapy targeting specific components of the immune response. Colectomy (partial or total removal of the large bowel through surgery) is occasionally necessary, and is considered to be a cure for the disease.

(I have a story to share in a bit.)

I remember taking the Betaseron accordingly and being so afraid of needles I would cry before every injection. I remember saying, "Oh My God! I have to do my needle in seven hours, then six hours, then five hours and so on.", and be so scared of the process I felt like I was having panic attacks. I would get my needle ready and say 1, 2, 3 and then chicken out, so I would have to build my courage up again—1, 2, 3, and I would wimp out again. This would sometimes go on for an hour or so. Then 1, 2, 3, I would inject it and the first thing in my head was knowing I would have to do this again in forty-eight hours and so the countdown would begin and the stress level would go up. (More on my Colitis later). I would sometimes have huge bruises or hit veins and bleed or even hit the muscle and have the wickedest Charlie horses. It was just complete hell every second day for me and this would carry on for about two years. I kept a journal of how I felt every day and my daily side effects. I finally decided to quit after nearly two years and I never took those injections again. Quite honestly I'm glad I made that decision.

I went back to work for about a year or so but my Multiple Sclerosis was tearing me apart fast. I was hurting all day, every day. My legs were cramping so badly and it seemed as if I was getting Charlie horses every five seconds. My work was suffering a great deal as a result so my boss decided to put me on long term disability. I guess he knew just how bad MS was as his Mom had suffered, and passed from it. I went downhill so fast, ending up with a cane within months, a walker within a year, and now I've been in wheelchair for the past five years.

Side note: Be very educated on your company benefits for disability (long term and short term) and how they can affect you directly. Make sure you are protected for life, disability and health benefits.

Life has been very difficult to deal with since being diagnosed. I was always active and playing sports in some way or another. To have it all taken away so fast is heartbreaking. I have often said, as awful as it may sound, I think it would have been better to have been given a terminal illness so you know what's happening and you have an idea when it may end. With Multiple Sclerosis you know it's going to get you sooner or later. You just don't have any idea of when or how. All you know is it's a waiting game, and that when it does come to get you, it's not going to be pretty. I hurt every day with pain, I cry every day, I fall, I cramp, I forget things, I have vision problems, I have sexual problems, I have a dead leg (won't move), I tingle from head to toe horribly and constantly, I have problems with my hands, (I can only use one finger to type with now, when it co-operates. Yes this whole book has been typed with just one finger—over 64,000 words which all comprise of single letters). I don't sleep very well. I have serious emotional issues, and I cry for no reason. I need to be cared for constantly—I am totally dependent. I'm sick and tired of my life as I am living it now.

And **I'm sick and tired of being sick and tired**.

Side note: Multiple Sclerosis affects everyone differently, some may never have an issue with Multiple Sclerosis and some may have to deal with it differently. This is how my Multiple Sclerosis is affecting me and my life. Being educated may help you be prepared for what may come. I say plan for the worst while hoping for the best.

I think the first MS symptoms I may have had were way back in grade six or seven.

The Spasticity:

I remember my legs always bouncing up and down like they were out of control.

Everybody used to tell me to stop bouncing them but I couldn't. They would just shake violently. They would shake under the kitchen table so uncontrollably that the plates, cups and everything on the table would bounce. When I was in school and the spasticity would start, my legs would shake my desk so much that I once had a teacher tie my legs to the chair as she thought I was goofing around. I actually fell over and she left me there for the whole class. I believe I shared this story at the beginning of my book.

I could literally bounce a baby to sleep on my lap. (It is too bad I couldn't harness that energy and make electricity. I would definitely be rich.)

It was like I was drumming but with no drums. If I was driving and stopped at a set of lights or stop sign they would start bouncing. I can always remember the cramping in them like a Charlie horse. I remember riding my bikes and them bouncing when I would stop.

I write this section as I find it important that we recognize any possible symptoms which may have been an indication of MS taking up residence in us. It may have merit or it may not. Always trust your own body, pay attention to it and

"If in doubt—check it out"

We are all different people with different symptoms representing different issues, but we are also all connected somehow.

Now back to the Colitis issue as it all ties together.

I remember the Colitis caused me to bleed heavily when I went to the washroom and I would feel as though I was going to pass out. Add to that the pain in my stomach which felt like a kick in the gut. I would have to run to the washroom thirty or forty times a day and definitely would never go out or go to restaurants because I was concerned I wouldn't be able to make it to the washrooms in time when necessary. I even slept in the washroom at home with a pillow on the sink, where I laid my head, because there was no sense going back to bed. I knew I would be back in the bathroom in another ten to fifteen minutes anyway. I remember praying for death several times because I just couldn't handle the pain anymore between the Multiple Sclerosis and Colitis and I felt like I was falling apart. This suffering continued for two more years. My wife finally had enough of seeing me go through this, called the Doctor and said, "That's it, no more. We need to do something now or he is going to die." She had me admitted to the hospital within a few hours and the doctors told us it was a very close call for me because I was in extremely bad shape and if we had left it much longer I could have died. I was in hospital for approximately three and a half weeks and lost over fifty pounds. I went into the hospital weighing almost one hundred and ninety-five pounds and came out at a weight of one hundred and forty-two pounds. My colon was removed because it was so severely damaged by the Colitis. The end result: I now have a Colostomy for the rest of my life.

I remember a time after my surgery and my stomach had not yet healed. I had about sixty stitches/staples inside and outside of my stomach. They were removed ten days later and I guess they had been taken out too soon. I went to bed and awoke a short time later to see I was covered in blood. My stomach had burst open as it seems the staples were taken out to soon. We rushed off to the hospital where I knew I was going to end up getting more staples to close my stomach so I was telling myself, "I'm going to get a needle and its okay.", over and over again to calm myself down. (I was however panicking as you know how much I hate, yes hate, needles). I went into the room, laid down on the table to get ready and I told the nurse, "I'm afraid of needles so please don't let me see it." Well, she started to talk with Arlette and she was so deep into the conversation she started to wave the needle around in the air. I saw it and said, "Look what you did! Now I can't take the needle to freeze it." After all the time I had spent getting ready by telling myself it would be okay these two gabbers got me back into my panicky state. The nurse said we needed to clean up the wound and redo the staples and that she needed to freeze it as it would be excruciatingly painful for me. I told her it was her fault and now I'd have to do it with no freezing because I wasn't going to have a needle(s). She said "WHAT? You're crazy!" I said, "Yep, just do it!" With that said, she started the procedure. She had to cut through muscle and tissue and go deep into my stomach to clean it out. Arlette sat there looking into my stomach and enjoying what she was seeing, sort of educational for her I guess. The nurse had to use a bunch of packing and gauze pads to clean the wound area and poured an antiseptic all over it and man that hurt so bad. She cleaned it, stitched me up, got me ready to go home and said she had never seen anyone do that and not scream to high heaven. I had to have nursing staff come to my home to take care of the wound every day. I do have pictures but I didn't think they would be appropriate to add here. Moral of the story: Stop talking and get the needles taken care of first!! Ha! Ha!

A life was given back to me after this as I now had a bit of hope that I could go out and be a functioning part of society, but the Multiple Sclerosis would rear its ugly head and take me out again. I had a massive attack and was put into the hospital once more. This one would wipe me out for good. I remember needing the wheelchair to get around. I came home and we had to have CCAC (Community Care Access Centre) visit me to assess my status and start the process of getting me what I needed. First it was the walker for Five Hundred Dollars and I couldn't believe it. What? Five Hundred Dollars for a walker? I planned for the worst but hoped for the best. I planned right. So not only did I have to deal with Multiple Sclerosis and Ulceritive Colitis, here I was having to deal with the financial costs as well. How was I going to do it? How were we going to do it?

My wife has always supported me but it is still like being alone because you don't want to keep crying or complaining as it you know it is becoming tiring to listen to the same complaints after a while, much like listening to a kid whine non-stop which is not fun. (I know because we have three boys!) I tried so hard to deal with what was happening to me, but it was so very difficult at times. (It still is!) I simply couldn't control or manage my body. I went into a deep depression. I felt I could not handle anymore of this miserable life. I thought it was too tough to deal with and I even tried to commit suicide I had reached the breaking point. I remember holding about twenty morphine pills and a glass of water in my hands. I was ready to take them and go to bed for the final time. I was on the verge of crying just before taking them because I was thinking about my family and everyone else in my life. At that very moment my son came around the corner and asked me if I was all right. That shook me up. Oh my God, I was just about to take my own life and my son is standing right there in front of me. At that very moment! I had forgotten about everyone and the effect this selfish act would have upon each of them. How stupid was I?

I immediately threw the pills in the sink and went crying to my wife. I broke down, told her what I had almost done and she let me have it but I was happy to hear her voice and thought of what I had just nearly done. I had almost destroyed a great family because I was in a bad place. My wife always seemed to get me out of my despair and I promised I would go to her before anything like this ever happened again. She threw the rest of the pills out and all the other medication we had in the house. I definitely was in a bad place with my MS and I needed to find a way to cope with it.

One of my wife's sayings to me is '**TOGETHER THERE IS NOTHING WE CAN'T DO**' and I took this literally. I have a tattoo of this saying on the top of my left hand so I see it every day and I always make sure to kiss it to remember her strength and what she has done for me. I have a banner below it and the letters MS so I always know it's there and we will fight for our lives together. As I said earlier, I often say my wife is two wings shy of being an angel and this is so true. She is my life, my best friend, my support system, my counsellor, my shrink, my mentor, my God, my everything. My life would not be complete without her. She and our boys are my life.

I have battled my MS for a long time. I've wanted to get an outside view, thoughts and opinions of what I can do to battle this disease living in me. I am looking for someone like me.

It is funny how many people have MS (approximately 75,000 Canadians alone at last count) but apparently we are all different and our individual MS is apparently so different from each others, but you know what—we are all the same in one way or another. We have an illness that affects our families the same. It tears them apart and everyone suffers for it in some way or another. My kids suffer every day. They see me fall, they see me cry, they see me hurt, they hear me yell and scream at my body, they see me hurt myself because I'm in so much pain, they see me deteriorate and yes their lives have been changed because of me. How many kids do you know that have to help lift their father when he falls in the bathtub or onto the floor? How many kids have to help their parent go to the washroom because he can't move? Mine do. We need gadgets and wheelchairs, walkers, canes, stair lifts, elevators, raised toilets, grab bars, modified showers, beds, chairs, rooms and many more things and this isn't going to affect the kids? Are you kidding me? They need to see a counsellor because of me and my disease. I've been in so much pain at times that not even a total of twenty-two Tylenol 3's taken in one day did anything to dull the pain. This constant suffering and chronic pain in a household is too much for any family to endure.

I remember one day I wanted to source out additional information regarding my MS. I was at my Doctor's office and someone mentioned they had just heard of a goalie in university who has MS and he still played hockey. I said, "WHAT?" I couldn't believe what I heard. I played hockey. Maybe he has or knows about something that I could do so I could function at a better state. I needed to find this person and learn what he was doing that enabled him to continue playing hockey. I found out where he was playing and contacted the training staff to find out what he did, what his diet was and anything else he was doing that helped him. He contacted me himself and I was amazed by his strength and determination. I kept in touch with him. He was my idol and my support through the toughest time in mine and my family's life. We talked via email many times. I was truly inspired by him and looked up to him in a major way. I watched him play at Bowling Green University and also with the AHL affiliate of the Boston Bruins, The Providence Bruins. He was an amazing inspiration to me and I wanted to be just like him. I wanted to be able to help someone else the way he helped me. I wanted to work and possibly even play hockey again. But this would not happen for me.

I remember seeing the schedule of the Providence Bruins one day and seeing that they were going to be playing in Rochester, New York against the Rochester Americans. It was the closest they came to Canada that year. I called the ticket office and told them I needed eight tickets right beside the Bruins bench first row section. (The girl thought I was crazy, here they are in Rochester, New York and this guy wants tickets beside the opposing team's bench). I bought all the tickets and then started planning a road trip. We went to Rochester and it was a trip that would change my life forever. We arrived for the game around five o'clock in the afternoon and took our seats. I saw my new friend, who was my inspiration, during his warm ups and managed to speak with him some more before his game. I remember he went into the dressing room and I was watching the Zamboni driver when I heard my name being called, "Hey, Mark!" I looked down and he threw me his jersey and told me that together we would shutout MS. I was absolutely floored he did this for me and, while I have a lot of jerseys, I cherish this jersey as one of my favourites. I thought to myself that here he is playing hockey with this miserable disease and I just knew, in that moment, I wanted to do something more with my life. I remember asking myself what could I do for MS? I thought and thought about it. What did I know? All I knew was hockey, business and accounting. So I started to brainstorm with my friend who came to the game with us. I had an idea of putting together a hockey tournament for MS and by the time we reached the Canadian border on our way home, I had a name and a great idea for it. I would host a ball hockey and ice hockey tournament for MS. I came up with the name. We Shoot . . . We Score . . . A Cure for MS (Ball and Ice hockey tournament) and started to plan how we could do it. I was on the Board of Directors with the MS Society so I approached them with my idea. They loved it.

They asked me to prepare a budget for it which I did. We had estimated we could raise Ten Thousand Dollars.

I started planning the event with a friend and we did a fantastic job together. We got in touch with many great people to help us make this event outstanding. I began to get teams interested in playing and some wonderful people came on board. The tourney was held in July, 2007 and we were able to raise over Thirteen Thousand Dollars for MS. We were all amazed that a one day tournament did so well. Although our friendship eventually drifted apart our joint venture stayed intact.

I started planning the second event on my own shortly after we finished the first one and the plan was for it to be bigger and better. To my astonishment, it was also going to turn out to be more troublesome than I could have ever imagined.

The MS Society became very demanding about wanting to run the tourney themselves. They wanted my contacts and were being very adamant about it. I remember asking during a board meeting, "What do you guys know about hockey or running a tournament of this magnitude?" Their reply was that they needed to be able to control it. I was not impressed with their attempt to take the tourney over. I had created it, worked so hard on it and now I was expected to just hand it over to other people so they could try to take care of it. I said NO and that was the beginning of the end, or so they thought. We had budgeted that Five Thousand Dollars was going to be held in trust from the last tournament to help offset the costs of the upcoming tournament in 2008. I began the planning and had all the teams interested in coming back along with the celebrities who came for the first tournament, Johnny Bower, Dickie Duff and others. I was very excited that we were going to do it again and it looked like it would be bigger and better as planned. I worked on the tourney the entire year unaware the biggest bombshell was about to be dropped on my head.

The MS Society's Chairman of our local chapter was starting to withhold information from people, including myself and others on our board. He told me he was doing this because apparently I had told someone how I was dealing with my MS and he said that the board could be held liable for what I said. I asked him if he was nuts and then I asked him how the board would be liable if I shared what I was doing regarding MS with someone. We asked him to tell us who, and what was being said. He said he would release information when and if he felt it was required or necessary to do so. We all had a very big problem with that as it was unprofessional conduct and against policy. I, along with five others, demanded an explanation and an apology for the blatant disrespect and unprofessional conduct directed towards us failing which we would all resign from the Board of Directors. The apology never came so we handed in our resignation letters and moved on. The letters of resignation were **never** handed into the head office of the MS Society. They mysteriously disappeared. A couple of the people who resigned went back on the Board of Directors which I found unbelievable after everything that had occurred.

Back to the tournament.

The tournament was now considered a third party event. I was officially black listed with the MS Society and it was to become worse believe me. Approximately one month before the tournament they threatened to cancel the tournament right out from under me. I remember telling them that they couldn't! How could they do that after all the endless, difficult and committed work that had gone into the preparation for it. Well, three weeks before the tournament date they did exactly that! They pulled the plug, officially cancelling my tournament for MS. I felt it was a personal shot aimed directly at me and I was devastated. I had to call sponsors, teams, people, volunteers, celebrities and tell each of them the MS Society had backed out of the tournament both physically and financially and I could not run the tourney without their help. Their personal shot at me killed a dream. Not to mention my spirit. I cried for hours after that, thinking how I had just hurt so many people with Multiple Sclerosis. I would not be able to provide them with the special tournament and fund raising that had been planned.

My wife came in and told me "WE DON'T NEED THOSE PEOPLE. WE WILL DO IT ON OUR OWN!"

So she really is the inspiration behind our moving forward with this event. She may not know it but it was because of her I went ahead with my plans. We contacted all the people involved, the sponsors, teams, volunteers and celebrities. We explained what happened and most of them came on board again. We booked another facility and held our tourney for other causes, not the MS Society. I was so affected by what they did that I decided I would never personally support them again. I had done walks, bike rides, hockey tournaments, sold flowers and so many more things for the MS Society, helping to raise tens of thousands of dollars for them and this was the way they thanked me. No thank you! I was finished with them.

As the tournament was growing and we were coming back on track, we decided we would change the name and start our own charity. We changed the name to: **WE SHOOT . . . WE SCORE . . . A CURE FOR . . .** and held our event in June 2009. We raised Five Thousand Dollars so it was less than we had planned for but we did it our way. We made donations to several charities and we felt great about it. I thought we could do this and really make a difference in peoples' lives so we proceeded to move forward by trade marking everything and incorporating our new venture. STOP!!!! Another major problem comes up. I had created the website approximately one and a half years prior to our tournament and we were well on the way to setting up our new venture without the help of the MS Society, but we were to be put on hold once again. I received a letter stating that our chosen name was in trademark status already. I said, "WTF! Who did this?" I found out another person was trying to start his own charity and was using the name I had applied for as a third party slogan. I filed a letter of opposition to fight for this name and then we were told that if it went to court it may cost us upwards to Twenty Thousand Dollars to fight for it.

I felt this was money that is raised to help others and I didn't want to waste it to fight for a name. I contacted the user directly, told him we had been using it on a website for a while and asked if he checked it out before registering the name. His reply was no, he hadn't and he was sorry. We had filed for the trademark in June and the tourney was scheduled for the end of June of 2009, so we had a major problem with this. I never expected someone else would have taken that name. I talked about this situation to some of the people associated with our tourney and they told me that it was not the name that was responsible for our success, it was what we had done for the people as a result of the tourney. So I changed the name and the logo, trademarked it and thus began

WE PLAY . . . WE SCORE . . . A CURE FOR . . . (Helping others is our "GOAL") & (Playing it forward)

We have since grown the charity foundation to really represent what we wanted it to be in the beginning, which is helping others. We are going to put the FUN back in the seriousness of fundraising.

We also trademarked: **PLAYING IT FORWARD.**

It's what we do. Who needs the past?? We have the future.

Although I had fought for the MS Society for many years and ultimately made a decision to not support them again, the headaches of the MS Society were not to go away for they would come to fight me again.

Choosing My Religion

insert this section as this area is a major part of and one of the biggest struggles in my life.

After the death of my Grandfather I truly started to wonder if there was something more out there. I never really believed in God or anything for that matter as far as religion was concerned.

My Grandfather was never religious either, so why I questioned this I have no idea. He was the first real death in my family. I have had friends pass and as much as that hurt I never questioned religion for any of them.

(R.I.P to all my lost friends)

Just after my Grandfather passed and Arlette and I were married we moved to Malta as you remember and this was a very religious place. I was still very confused about my beliefs but always kept it to myself as I felt very strange about this part of my life. I remember being in churches and for whatever reason I felt very comfortable. Something peaceful was surrounding me it seemed. I learned some prayers but never really said them. I learned the sign of the cross, but always felt out of place doing it as I was not a Catholic.

I remember trying to pray to see what it was like, but didn't know what to do or say. So I always forgot about it. (It just seemed chaotic and confusing.)

I'm going to share a funny story about when I attended church once. I remember one of my first times going to a Catholic Mass. They have a part in the Mass where the Priest offers a sign of peace. "Peace be with you.", he says and asks you to offer a sign of peace to others. You would then shake the hands of those surrounding you and say, "Peace be with you." Being the rookie I was and really feeling the spirit of the Lord, I extended my hand to the congregation standing around me and said, "Pleased to meet you.", to each of them as I shook their hands, which was what I thought I heard the Priest say. Also, there was so much up and down, what with kneeling, praying, standing, sitting, then kneeling again I couldn't keep up with it. I knelt down and leaned forward to pray at one time only to butt heads with the elderly lady in front of me. Oh boy, was I off to a good start.'

I remember after we moved back to Canada in 1998 my Grandmother died and then it really started to mess with my mind. Is there something out there? My Grandmother was religious and prayed every day. She had given me bibles for Christmas and I always put them in the 'forgotten drawer'. That's where I put things I didn't care about.

I had questioned religion for quite some time and truly wondered if there was something more for me in this area. Was I being called, so to speak, and why was this leaning toward learning more about religion happening? I kept this to myself for a number of years and then in 2005 sometime I started in inquire about religion. I remember praying and asking God if this was for me? Was this what I wanted or what I needed? I finally decided yes, this was what I wanted. I was feeling something and wanted to explore it more.

I had been in churches both here and in Malta from time to time and each time I had felt a comfortable feeling being there so now I wanted to become part of it. I wanted to become Catholic and change my life for the better.

I remember talking to the Priest at the church we went to and sharing my feelings with him. He asked if I was being forced into this decision by anyone and I told him no, I wanted this for myself. I remember thinking this was truly something I really wanted for me. More than any material possession, I wanted to find God.

The Priest told me I had to go to classes before I could become Catholic and I needed a sponsor to be with me for the duration. A sponsor is someone who takes part in the journey with you and is of that chosen denomination (Catholic in this case).

I wondered who I could ask. I wanted someone who I respected and who would take me seriously as well as be willing to go through this journey with me. I decided to ask my sister-in-law and she said yes. So my journey began. I had to attend classes every week, take part in bible studies, attend church and even do exams so to speak. I loved it. I remember sitting in a class in the church, reading our bibles together and my having the strange calm feeling of peace inside me. I well remember the classes and the people who were on this journey with me. I was still the joker and had a sense of humour in an otherwise very serious environment though. I asked odd questions, such as, "If we are all children of God, why do they make such a fuss over Jesus?" But I did take it seriously and did quite well in my classes. I completed my teachings and was baptised as a Catholic. I felt so good and went to church regularly after that. I felt like my life would turn around for the better. Then I think I became worse medically and for whatever reason I stopped attending for a couple of weeks. After that it seemed that I simply stopped going to church.

I started to ask God, "God, why did you do this to me? What about the bad guys of this world?" Why did God have to do this to me? I began to build a lot of anger along with resentment and it seems I have never really released it. I needed someone to blame I think and God was going to be my target. I have struggled with my religion for some time since. I would give anything for a sign that all will be well but to date there has been nothing. I still pray in my head and ask for help. I pray for a pain free day every day, but nothing yet. I pray every day for help and the strength for my family to get through this extraordinary time of our lives.

I will hopefully be able to get my religion back and ask for forgiveness for doubting what I tried so hard to get . . . . God in my life.

My Attitude

My attitude has always been 'FTW' and those who don't like it can jump in a lake basically. I would think of saying, "Hi. I'm Mark. How do you like me so far? And if you don't . . . don't waste my time." I think it may be worse more so now than ever as I cannot seem to control it any more (I'm sure it's the medication doing its damage as well).

I have always felt that the world was against me in some way and now here I am battling this disease with the constant pain and agony fast winning. I literally give up. '**FTW**' I say and let it be.

I'm tired of people being judgemental and saying, "It will be okay." or "I know how you feel." No, you don't know how I feel and no . . . it's not going to be okay!! I want a way out of the pain and the knowing that my body is going to get worse and there is nothing I can do about it except wait. This truly sucks. I'm going to lose this fight and there is nothing I can say or do to stop it and then I have people wondering why my attitude is getting worse.

I have stopped caring about my health and my body when I should be caring more as I have a wife and kids who need me. It is just so hard to constantly hurt and be a happy parent or husband.

I think I have lost the passion for life and so my attitude grows stronger, but in a negative way.

I have checked myself out of the hospital more times than you can imagine. If I thought alcohol and drugs would help I would be an alcoholic drug addict big time.

A funny story about my attitude . . . I once got pulled over by the police for a seatbelt violation and I was upset. He stopped me on one of my bad days and now he was about to hear about it. He asked me if I knew why he had pulled me over and I replied that he must have failed in school and this was the best job he could get and now he was trying to meet his quota for the day. He wrote me a ticket but I wasn't going to sign it just to get him going. I did sign it finally after uttering a few more choice words and then drove off after he handed me the ticket. Well, his lights came on again and

I was only fifteen feet away from him. I thought he forgot to give me my licence back so I stopped my car and waited for him. He strutted up to my window where I held out my hand expecting my licence to be handed back to me. He asked me if I knew why he stopped me again and I told him because he had forgotten to give me back my license for which he replied, "Nope. You forgot to put your seatbelt on." and he promptly wrote me another ticket. FTW. If you wonder why I have an attitude, look at my life. It's hard to go through this life without developing one. I have a heart of gold and would do anything for anyone, but get me angry and "**clap on**" my light switch goes on accompanied by my attitude. It seems uncontrollable even when I try to stop it.

CCSVI

In November, 2009 I was watching a television show with my family and friends on Multiple Sclerosis and we thought, 'Oh my God, there is a possible cure for Multiple Sclerosis." This was called CCSVI which stands for Chronic Cerebro-Spinal Venous Insufficiency. A description follows:

Chronic Cerebro-Spinal Venous Insufficiency (CCSVI) is a term used to describe compromised flow of blood in the veins draining the central nervous system. It has been hypothesized to play a role in the cause of multiple sclerosis (MS) This hypothesis was first put forth by Paolo Zamboni in 2008. An endovascular intervention for the syndrome has been attempted however further research is required to determine if the benefits outweigh the risks of the procedure.

The hypothesis and procedure has generated optimism among people with MS but received skepticism from the majority of the medical community as the procedure may lead to serious complications while its benefits have not been proven. In addition concern has been raised with Zamboni's research as it was neither blinded nor controlled and further studies in 2010 and 2011 had variable results. This has raised serious objections to the hypothesis of CCSVI originating in multiple sclerosis. Additional research efforts investigating the CCSVI hypothesis are underway.

This would possibly give people with MS a fighting chance against the disease which has taken me down so fast. I started to study everything about CCSVI and was very interested in having this surgery done for myself. I remember hearing the constant negative comments by the MS Society and it was annoying me to no end because I was with the MS Society and somehow just felt there was not as much care put forward as I would have like to see for people with MS. I remember calling the neurologist I dealt with in Toronto as well and telling him I felt like he didn't care about people with MS either and I wasn't going to use him anymore and I didn't. I was on my own again to fight this disease and fight it I would.

I remember the annual walk for MS was coming up in April, 2010. I had always participated in these walks and had even been the Chairman of one of the walks. I had raised thousands of dollars for the MS Society and spent a lot of time, effort and much personal time away from my family while volunteering for this and other events.

I remember having so many problems with the MS Society and the new CCSVI discovery. I felt that the MS Society was flat out ignoring the needs of thousands of people with MS and their rights to be treated. The MS Society kept saying they needed more research, and more answers before moving forward with anything. I felt and still do that we, as MS'rs, have a right to make decisions for ourselves and we wanted to make very clear to them that that we wanted those choices made available. I made a sign for the back of my wheelchair that said

"I'D RATHER BE WALKING, BUT APPARENTLY THE MS SOCIETY WANTS US TO WAIT FOR MORE RESEARCH. I DON'T HAVE TIME TO WAIT. PLEASE SUPPORT CCSVI RESEARCH.

I went to the walk with my son and we were asked to leave because of my sign. I was told by the Chairman of the Board that we were ruining "**his walk**" and we were not welcome there. I told him I didn't realize it was "**his walk**". I was happy for him that he could walk but, as he could see, I couldn't. My son and I sat outside in the cold and rain until all the participants had gone in. They each had a chance to see my sign and hear my story of what had happened. I was interviewed by the local paper and TV station covering the event. I had my picture taken and displayed in the paper for all to see what had taken place. A lot of people were disgusted by this action that had taken place with me and said they would no longer support the MS Society. Actually some people even insisted that their donations go to CCSVI research. I collected my donations back and returned them to my contributors. The next page has more information on this.

Here below is the article written about me on May 5, 2010

MS rally demands treatment

Sad plight. Hundreds of people with Multiple Sclerosis rallied outside the Ontario legislature in Toronto Wednesday, to demand access to a procedure not available in Canada. Mark Stewart and his 10-year-old son were booted from a Brampton walk-a-thon recently for asking the MS Society of Canada to fund the treatment.

Some 150 Canadians including Brampton residents with multiple sclerosis (MS) rallied outside the Ontario legislature in Toronto Wednesday, to demand access to a procedure not available in Canada or covered by provincial health insurance policies.

The procedure, chronic cerebrospinal venous insufficiency —or CCSVI, has been put forward by an Italian doctor, Paolo Zamboni.

CCSVI is used to describe a situation in which the venous system is unable to efficiently remove blood from the central nervous system. Using vessel-opening techniques such as angioplasty—similar to that used to unblock clogged arteries that develop with heart disease—researchers have met with some success But many—neurologists and officials from the MS Society of Canada alike—are cautious and say a more thorough study is needed to determine the relationship between CCSVI and the disease.

A few weeks ago, Brampton resident Mark Stewart, 41, a MS patient, was booted from an annual walk-a-thon because of his criticism of the MS Society of Canada.

Stewart said the MS Society is wasting hundreds of thousands dollars on research grants to study the relationship between CCSVI and MS, when it should be directing the same funds to doctors performing the treatment.

In a release Wednesday, the Multiple Sclerosis Society of Canada, called on the federal government to provide $10 million for research into CCSVI and MS.

Many of the protesters at the rally are calling the Canadian health-care system to cover the diagnostic tests to look for blocked veins in people with MS.

Among them was a Brampton resident, whose husband suffers from MS.

"What brings me here today is my husband, He's had MS for 20 years and we have been trying all different things to see if we can get him walking again," she told Macleans. "His left side is gone completely, so we're hoping one day he'll be able to have this surgery they are saying could help to unclog the veins, and hopefully he'll be able to have some use of his left side again."

Rallies were planned for Halifax, Ottawa, Toronto, Regina, Edmonton, Vancouver, Victoria and other cities.

Here is article number two written on April 30, 2010

Man gets booted from MS Walk

Protest on wheels. Last week, Mark Stewart, 41, and his 10-year-old son arrived at the Terry Miller Recreation Centre to take part in the 2010 Brampton-Caledon MS Walk. They weren't allowed to take part because of a sign on Stewart's wheelchair.

A Brampton resident with multiple sclerosis (MS) who was not allowed to participate in an annual walk-a-thon because of his criticism of the MS Society of Canada has vowed to have his voice heard.

Last week, Mark Stewart, 41, and his 10-year-old son arrived at the Terry Miller Recreation Centre to take part in the 2010 Brampton-Caledon MS Walk.

On the back of Stewart's wheelchair was a sign that read he supports chronic cerebrospinal venous insufficiency (CCSVI) research, and if the MS Society supports the therapy, he might be able to walk again.

Because of the sign, an organizer would not let Stewart take part in the walk.

The term CCSVI is used to describe a situation in which the venous system is unable to efficiently remove blood from the central nervous system. Using vessel-opening techniques such as angioplasty—similar to that used to unblock clogged arteries that develop with heart disease—researchers have met with some success.

The technique made headlines last year after an Italian researcher published results of his ground-breaking work.

Right now, CCSVI offers a glimmer of hope for thousands of people with MS.

Stewart said while the MS Society hands out grants to multiple researchers for multi-year projects, he and others with MS will lose out because time, he said, is of essence.

Stewart's protest was directed at the MS Society of Canada, which he said is wasting hundreds of thousands dollars on research grants to study the relationship between CCSVI and MS, when it should be directing the same funds to doctors performing the treatment.

"MS Society wants to wait for more research even though there are doctors all over the world doing the surgery," said Stewart. "I'm in a wheel chair. I don't have another two years to wait for a study to be done. I want to walk again. I want to be a husband and father to my kids." The vice-president of the Ontario division of MS Society, said contrary to Stewart's beliefs, the organization strongly supports the research and is moving quickly to support CCSVI research.

The society maintains the CCSVI concept is still a hypothesis and is not a proven therapy for MS.

The relationship between CCSVI and MS needs to be studied, replicated and validated in much larger well-designed studies, she said.

She said she regrets the fact that Stewart was not allowed to participate in the fundraiser, saying the incident was a result of "two people passionate about MS." (At least I was)

"It was an unfortunate incident and I'm sorry Mark experienced the walk in that manner. It wasn't our intention," she said.

She said the MS Society of Canada is among the first in the world to open up its grant application process for research into CCSVI.

"The MS Society is wasting money," said Stewart, who has received support from hundreds of people on his Facebook page. "The slogan is End MS not wait for an end to MS.

We're on the on-ramp to the highway of MS . . . don't close the highway now."

I have fought for the rights of people with Multiple Sclerosis for years and will continue to do so. This was only the tip of the iceberg though. I went on the walk with a couple of people only to find it wasn't even a wheelchair accessible route. I made sure to make this a point. I have been shut out by the MS Society many times since then and will continue to fight them until the end. I told them I believed a complete rebuild was and is needed to do it right and NO I don't want to be on the Board of Directors again. I just want to see it done right, for the people by the people.

Multiple Sclerosis is so expensive and people deserve the right to be able to obtain the items they need at a decent price and at a good place. The MS Society should give one hundred percent of its resources to MS patients, but I find that most of the information I get is from my wife's researching the illness and looking for resources. I have found that the following have been very helpful and should be looked into.

Community care access centre (CCAC) for home nursing care, physiotherapy, occupational therapists and more. www.ccac-ont.ca

The March of dimes (They can offer funding for special home and vehicle modifications needed) www.marchofdimes.ca

Assistive devices program ADP. They can help with funding of items that may be needed. http://www.health.gov.on.ca/english/public/program/adp/adp_mn.html

Disability credits on **income tax**. Check with your accountant.

CPP. Canada pension plan. (If you're in Canada) http://www.servicecanada.gc.ca/eng/isp/cpp/cpptoc.shtml

ODSP Ontario disability support program http://www.mcss.gov.on.ca/en/mcss/programs/social/odsp/contacts/index.aspx

Also check with your local members of Parliament, Ward councillors and even your Mayor if needed.

And always check with **local charities** for extra assistance.

The local **MS Society** offers programs for equipment funding, cleaning, transportation ETC. but you have to do the research to find what else they can offer.

And last but not least, your family doctor can help you find assistance as well. Also find a support group. This can be helpful too or talk to someone with Multiple Sclerosis as you will be amazed at what they know, have or are experiencing and are willing share with you.

THE MERIDA EXPERIENCE

I remember begging to have this new surgery in order to give me a chance against Multiple Sclerosis but as always the MS Society would not consider it when I requested it. My body had deteriorated so much during the following two months that we began to think that even this surgery wouldn't work for me. My wife researched and investigated into so many options that might provide me with this procedure that it became crazy. She finally announced she had found the place and now all we needed was the money. Next challenge! She decided with a good friend that we could do a Fundraiser to raise the money and that is exactly what we did. The Fundraiser was scheduled for October, 2010, but my body was breaking down so quickly at this point that we knew I may not last until then. My wife's employer stepped up to the plate for us big time. He told us if we needed the money right away he would give it to us and we could pay him back from the Fundraiser that was going to be held. Then he told us that if we didn't raise the necessary funds that this would be his gift to us and not to worry. He gave me the gift of life and a fighting chance against Multiple Sclerosis. My wife booked my surgery in Merida, Mexico and we were getting all our eggs in one basket so to speak. Our families were questioning our every move, but they were just being concerned. Even up to the day before we left we were being questioned. One thing I have always had is total trust in my wife and any decision she makes. I don't even give it a second thought. I trust her with my life.

Arlette is someone who looks into everything and doesn't make rash or quick decisions (that's me—rash and quick decisions). My Dad wanted to go with us but his holidays would not coincide with our trip. My brother said he would come with us and thank God he did, because this was not going to be an easy trip. August 25th at three o'clock in the morning we woke up and started to get ready for our six o'clock departure. We arrived at the airport in Toronto on time, booked in and packed my wheelchair into a bag to go on the plane for transit to Merida. I had to use an airport wheelchair and they are not that comfortable, believe me. My brother wheeled me all the way through the airport to security where they checked us thoroughly. Then we sat and waited for our flight. We sat at the terminal waiting for our jumbo jet to Havanna, Cuba where we would be transferring to another flight to Mexico. Well, this small plane pulls up to our terminal and we thought he was lost. Turns out he wasn't. This small plane was indeed our flight, and I began wondering how I was going to fit in there. I needn't have worried. They wheeled me down and put me in my seat. We took off a bit late because of having to get me organized and settled in. Then we had a rough flight which became worse, much worse. We landed in Havanna, Cuba. The people came to get me with a wheelchair that was missing an arm rest and I was wheeled into the airport. The security guard asked us to hand over our passports as we were transferring onto a Mexico flight and they would be returned to us, which we did. We went into the airport and my God it looked like the world had simply forgotten about this place. It was unbelievable. The roof was leaking and they had garbage cans set up to catch the water which were now over flowing. Birds were flying around inside the airport and landing on the countertops where the food was being prepared. I had ordered lunch and a bird came down and took a piece of the bread that was being used to make my sandwich. The girl grabbed another piece of bread and was going to give me the same sandwich the bird had pecked at. She saw me look at her and ended up making me another one. Then I had to go to the washroom and there was a guy who didn't speak a word of English sitting in the washroom like a clerk or something. They had no handicapped washroom stalls, or even seats on the toilets and the guy was there to give you pieces of toilet paper as you needed them. "WTF", came to mind and I decided I would hold it until I got to Mexico. I wanted to get out of there as quickly as possible. The Customs people still had our passports and I was starting to get concerned, and angry. Cuba is certainly not a place that would take my temper too well. I asked them what they were doing with our passports and they told me they would have them brought back to us shortly. Three hours later they were finally returned to us.

I remember our plane to Mexico was parked on the tarmac and we couldn't find the gate to get to it. The airport staff left a lot to be desired and after much inquiry as to how to get to it, and no answers, we decided to find it for ourselves. We went down towards the terminal gate that we thought might be the right one and asked if that was where we were to catch the flight to Mexico. The guy looked at me with a strange expression. I guess he had never seen someone in a wheelchair before because he looked so confused. We were informed they needed to get me transported to the plane which was on the tarmac and not at a terminal gate. (There were only three of them and they weren't open.) They told Arlette and my brother to board the plane and I would be brought out later when the ambulance that would transport me arrived. (Yes, they were going to put me in an ambulance to take me to the plane to board.) I waited for about twenty-five minutes by myself in a basement terminal in Cuba. I finally went outside towards the tarmac and saw the plane sitting there. They were waiting for me and I had no ride to the plane. I asked if I could just wheel myself over to the plane and board. They told me no and that I had to wait for the ambulance. It was coming. Then this aged cargo van pulls up and I asked if that was their ambulance to which they responded resoundingly, "Yes. Why?" WHY? For one reason it was all white and rusty with no medical signs or lights on it indicating it was an ambulance. It actually had rust holes in it, and it looked like the door was going to fall off the passenger side. Two guys get out of the vehicle and come toward me with a dolly truck with a seat on it. (Duct taped to it I must add.) They asked me to come off the curb and to stand on the dolly truck. Incredible! I said, "Do you see the wheelchair? I can't walk!"

They finally helped me onto the dolly truck and literally taped me to it. One of them lifted the bottom, the other one held the handrail and they proceeded to slide me into this ambulance that looked like it came right out of the 'Texas Chainsaw Massacre'. The inside was below any standards I had ever seen. It had a wooden bench with a piece of plywood and blanket on it that was their "stretcher". The cabinet had fish hooks on it and it was totally rusted out. They shut the door and I could still see the outside through rust holes in the door. This is what an ambulance in Cuba looks like?

209

They drove me out to the plane and had this look on their faces when we arrived that seemed to be saying, "What? We have to get him up there too?" There were about eight stairs leading up to the plane's entrance. Remember they parked on the tarmac. So these two guys pushed me out of the ambulance and started to bounce me up the stairs with a bang~bang~ bang! Up I went and when we got to the entrance of the plane one of the guys says, "Boy, you are one fat American. We should get a tip for this!" I told him to consider it customer service. They banged me the rest of the way into the plane and got me near the seats, at which time they cut me loose, one grabbed my feet, one grabbed me under the arms and together they threw me onto the seats. Yes they literally threw me over one seat to the inside window seat. I almost fell onto the floor as they walked away and did not help me get seated. I could not see my brother or my wife. I leaned myself over and saw they were at the back of the plane, so now I was sitting up here by myself. The plane ride was so stressful as there was a great deal of turbulence. I could not believe it. Now this!! I tried to sleep on the flight but my head kept hitting the window. I recall the plane felt like it dropped out of the sky for a moment. It dropped what felt like two thousand feet in two seconds and there was a loud banging sound. I heard my wife scream. They were right at the back of the plane near the washroom, so I hoped it was the toilet seat that had slammed shut and was making that noise. I was so scared I was going to die and here I was with my wife sitting at the rear of the plane and I wouldn't even get to be with her.

We finally made it to Mexico and pulled up to the terminal to go into the airport. There was a person who met us with a wheelchair and wheeled me to where we needed to go. He took us to customs, waited with us to get our papers sorted out and then wheeled me to the luggage rack where my wheelchair was waiting. He helped us unpack and set it up and finally walked us to the front doors where our contact was waiting. We gave him a generous tip for his kind and accommodating service. Our taxi driver was waiting for us and we headed off to the hotel. We arrived at the hotel about twenty-five minutes later. The sun was shining brightly and it was hot. I mean hot—the temperature was near forty degrees. We went up to our room and just relaxed for a bit, not quite believing we made it, but we had.

My brother was a God send to us on this trip. Everywhere we went or anything we did my brother had to lift me in or out of my wheelchair, into the taxi van or up and down curbs. We decided to go out for a bite to eat and found a Burger King there, so we went in for dinner and returned to the hotel to relax. The next morning we were going to head out for breakfast but the extreme heat got to me and we had to go back to the hotel room. I believed I was suffering with heat stroke. About twenty minutes later my wife said the Doctor told her we could go over to the hospital for my tests so off we went for them. It was less than fifty yards away for which we were very thankful. They did my MRV, blood tests along with other tests and just as we were about to leave the Doctor came over and told us my surgery could be done immediately if I wanted. I told him yes, because I wanted to get it over with. I was terrified and told my wife I loved her so much because I didn't know what to expect. My surgery was scheduled for six o'clock that evening. I can remember the nurse putting the gas mask on me and I began counting down backwards from ten so I could go to sleep. But after 10-9-8-7-6-5-4-3-2-1 I wasn't asleep, so I repeated the countdown. 10-9-8-7-6-5-4-3-2-1 and again I wasn't asleep. I became a little worried so told myself that I would count down one more time and if that didn't work I would tell the nurse I still wasn't asleep. (I felt like I was in the movie 'Awake' where the guy had surgery while he was actually awake but he was paralyzed and couldn't tell them he hadn't fallen asleep.) I counted again and nothing happened. Then I heard the nurse say, "We are done, Mark. Wake up." I thought. "What? I'm still counting down." They were laughing when I came to and the Doctor told me I had counted backwards from ten for almost two hours while they were doing the surgery. I wasn't totally asleep but thought I was supposed to be. My surgery went very well and I was transferred up to my hospital room for the night to rest and to be monitored. I remember Arlette and my brother being there when I awakened and he had brought me M&M's, my favourite candy of all time. My right hand had been almost seized closed because of the MS prior to the surgery and now here I was easily picking up one M&M with my right hand.

We were all so excited when we saw my right hand was working. I had no pain in my legs either which I had suffered with non-stop for many years and my feet were back to a normal color. I was still very groggy from the medication so it was now time for sleep. My wife stayed in the room with me for the night while my brother went back to the hotel for a good night's sleep. I kept waking up Arlette throughout the night to ask her what time it was. The next morning I was released by nine o'clock and we decided to go for breakfast. I think the temperature was about forty-three degrees and I loved it. Interesting. The day before I thought I had heat stroke and now I here I was loving the heat. We ate and went back to the room where I sat on the balcony sun tanning for a couple of hours. It rained very hard in the afternoon but I sat in the rain, something else I could never do. I was so excited for having had the surgery as now I felt like I was a re-born person. We met others from Canada while we were in Mexico and still keep in touch with them. We spent three extra days in Mexico which enabled us to do some sightseeing and visit the bars for dinner ('stay thirsty my friends'—a favourite saying of ours there). I hadn't had a beer in nearly ten years so it was a nice treat to have one in Mexico.

The people were great and the locals were wonderful to us. They tried so hard to break the language barrier and were very friendly. We went to Wal-Mart, Burger King, Boston Pizza and Chilie's, we saw Blockbuster, 711, and a number of other American stores. We went to the Gulf of Mexico, saw other beautiful sights and enjoyed the people so it was amazing for us.

We left on the Sunday morning and headed home. We were going through Mexico City this time, not Havanna, so we were very happy. We boarded the plane and off we went, leaving beautiful Merida, Mexico behind us along with the great people and friends we met. Mexico City airport was like nothing I had ever seen before. It was immense in size. The flight was rough so we were happy to be on the ground again. The people met us with a wheelchair and took us to our terminal. Remember I said the airport was big, right? We had to take a train inside the airport to our terminal and it took us about ten minutes to get there. The airport employee pushed me the entire way, through everything, to get us to where we were going. He was super to do that because that would have been difficult for Arlette or my brother to do. We sat and had lunch (Subway and Chinese food) and then went to our gate to await our flight home. We boarded the Air Canada flight to come home and again they were very accommodating. They brought me to my seat first which was in section twenty-three, so it took a bit of time to get me settled in but everyone was patient. Then we took off. Up, up and away. Homeward bound. Our flight was about five hours long and we arrived back in Toronto around five o'clock in the afternoon. Our trip to Mexico was absolutely amazing in every way and we would certainly recommend Merida to anyone.

I started into physiotherapy shortly after we got home and was beginning to get better. I was learning to walk a bit with my walker and my entire body was just feeling so much better. We were also still planning our fundraiser for October and we were both looking forward to the next chapter of our lives.

Our fundraiser was held in October, 2010. We raised enough money to cover the surgery and the flights plus we had some funds remaining for my physiotherapy as it was going to be long road to travel for me to become mobile again.

Well, here we are approximately one year and four months after my surgery and I'm sorry to say the surgery did not work for me. My body has gone back to the way it was and is in constant pain again. The anger has returned with a vengeance and the feeling of complete failure exists in me every day. I wanted this so much but like so many things in my life a wall has been put up in front of me. How do I get over this one?

I keep falling and having to call 911 as my family can't pick me up. I sleep in a chair because I can't get on my bed and this is devastating to me. My body cramps and goes into seizures so often that I feel and look like I am a fish out of water thrashing about. We are struggling to get the help we need to take care of me and I truly sense the nursing home is coming soon.

An article was written about me in the newspaper shortly after we returned from having my surgery in 2010. Here it is as written by The Brampton Guardian.

Row over MS treatment

Free from pain. Brampton resident Mark Stewart, 41, pictured here with son Dylan, 3, traveled to Mexico recently where he underwent a controversial procedure that helps curb the debilitating pain brought on by multiple sclerosis, a condition he's had for the last eight years. The procedure was developed by an Italian doctor last year and has since become the centre of a huge debate among patients, Canadian health officials and politicians.

Mark Stewart, 41, has regained a level of freedom he hasn't possessed in a really long time.

"I have been in a wheelchair for years but look, I can stand," gestured the Brampton resident, showing the results of a recent trip to Mexico where he underwent a controversial procedure for multiple sclerosis (MS). "I haven't been able to lift my arms in eight years and look, I can do that now. For me this is such a huge thing."

Diagnosed with MS eight years ago, Stewart's body became a prison over time.

Living with the disease confined him to a wheelchair and prevented him from doing the things he loves most in life, like play hockey or being active with his young children Jason, 10, Randy, 14, and Dylan, 3.

So, when the father of three heard of a procedure that treats MS by opening blocked veins in the upper body, he was eager to cover the $9,800 price tag and head off to Mexico in late August to try it.

Stewart feels the money was well spent, even though Canada's healthcare establishment isn't yet convinced that this new "liberation treatment" is the real deal.

"The government wants people to wait for the research? Well, I can tell you my body couldn't wait anymore. I was in too much pain," Stewart said. "This procedure works and I'm proof of that."

The Canadian Institute for Health Research (CIHR) and the MS Society of Canada met in Ottawa last month to discuss research priorities for the debilitating neurological disease, for which there is no cure.

At the meeting, leading medical and scientific experts decided unanimously to recommend against funding mass nationwide clinical trials for the procedure without first taking a closer look at whether it actually works.

"The experts agreed that there is an overwhelming lack of scientific evidence on the safety and efficacy of the procedure," They said there is not enough evidence to link MS to blocked veins.

"The experts concluded that given this lack of scientific basis, it was neither scientifically advisable nor ethically acceptable to conduct a therapeutic clinical trial on this procedure at this time," The federal agency recommended that Ottawa set up a scientific working group to analyze and monitor the results of a handful of studies currently being undertaken before moving ahead, a recommendation that has infuriated proponents of the procedure.

Stewart, for one, said he is living proof that the treatment is legitimate and is critical of those who would deny MS patients in Canada from receiving the treatment here.

He said some people just don't have the time to wait around for the government to ponder the results of clinical trials.

"Why would Canada deny people this?" Stewart asked.

Italian medical professor and former vascular surgeon Dr. Paolo Zamboni pioneered the treatment.

It is based on a theory that a condition called CCSVI (chronic cerebrospinal venous insufficiency) causes narrowed neck veins, which leads to iron deposits to build up and damage brain cells.

Zamboni believes unblocking the veins—a routine angioplasty is used to clear up clogged jugular veins—can help MS sufferers.

Angioplasty is available to Canadians with different medical problems, but is specifically off limits to MS patients.

Those who want the treatment must travel to other countries like Mexico, India and Bulgaria, and pay for it themselves.

For Stewart, the decision to undergo the surgery was immediate.

After catching a television program last November featuring the liberation treatment, Stewart and his wife Arlette began researching the procedure on the Internet.

Their search led the couple to a vascular imaging clinic in Barrie that offers testing for CCSVI.

Dr. Sandy McDonald, a vascular surgeon and director of the Barrie clinic, determined Stewart was a prime candidate for the procedure.

However, due to Ottawa's stance on the liberation treatment, McDonald advised Stewart he wouldn't be able to get it done in Canada.

Undeterred, the family continued their hunt for a facility that performed the procedure and eventually found a facility in Mexico.

MY STORY FROM M TO S

Stewart arrived in the coastal city of Mérida on Aug. 24 and within 24 hours was treated and released from hospital.

"Aug. 25 is my new birthday," said Stewart, as his eyes well up with tears. "My birthday is in February but I consider that day (Aug. 25) my birthday now. It was the start of a new life for me."

Stewart can't exactly lace up his skates at this point, but his health has improved to such a degree that he says even doctors are amazed.

Moving his arms up and down was impossible before treatment.

Also, the feeling in his legs has returned and for the first time in years, the Brampton resident can fully open up his right hand.

His doctors expect him to be wheelchair-free within six months, he said.

"It's like I have a new husband," Stewart's wife Arlette said. "The results of (the treatment) have been amazing. It's like he's reborn."

Health ministers across the country have been grappling with whether to fund their own studies into the theory since the new procedure popped up last year.

Last week, Canada's health minister Leona Aglukkaq backed recommendations put forth by the CIHR and MS Society that an expert scientific working group be created to monitor studies already underway.

Aglukkaq said Canada would move forward with countrywide trials as soon as she receives findings from seven research projects announced in May.

She said preliminary results are expected within a few months.

The decision by the federal government to hold off on clinical trials has drawn mixed reactions from MS patients.

Stewart is critical of the government for its stance, arguing the only way to clear up questions about the treatment is to fund high-quality trials. While others, like Michael Augustine, welcomed the more cautious approach that Health Canada decided to take.

"You're asking someone with multiple sclerosis if he wants to get better. Of course I want to get better," Augustine, who received his diagnosis 18 years ago, told The Toronto Star. "Do I want to harm myself in the process? Absolutely not."

But some provinces are taking matters into their own hands.

Saskatchewan said it would accept proposals for clinical trials, while Newfoundland plans to spend $320,000 for neurologists to observe patients from that province who have had the treatment done in other countries.

Ontario has decided not to proceed with clinical trials.

The Zamboni technique has become a highly controversial and divisive issue, pitting patients against doctors and even patients against the MS Society.

Stewart, who has raised money for the MS Society for years, said he is frustrated with the organization because he feels it is not fighting hard enough for patients who want access to treatment in Canada.

The family spent $9,800 to have the procedure done in Mexico when it would have cost a fraction of that (about $1,500) had it been performed here.

Stewart said he was lucky to secure the money for Mexico, but there are many Canadians that aren't so fortunate.

Although the MS Society has donated millions of dollars for research into liberation therapy, it will not endorse clinical trials in Canada.

That's because the theory behind it "is neither dismissible nor refuted, but it is also not proven", said the society's president and CEO of the MS society. There is far from consensus in the medical community as to whether Zamboni's theory has merits.

Mark Stewart believes the controversy just emphasizes the importance of moving to clinical trials as soon as possible.

This article was written in the Brampton Guardian on September 20, 2010.

I'm still a strong believer in this procedure even though it did not totally work for me. Would I do it again? **HELL YES.** I feel this surgery is very important to someone with the beginning stages of Multiple Sclerosis and should be made available so we can decide for ourselves whether to do it or not.

We Play . . . We Score . . . A Cure For . . . ™

s you may remember from earlier in the book the tournament name was started as

WE SHOOT . . . WE SCORE . . . A CURE FOR MS . . . and we had issues with the MS Society so we went our separate ways and became **We Shoot . . . We Score . . . A Cure for . . .** but then we had some issues with someone who took our name. While at the time we were initially upset with what had occurred, we do wish him well and all the success in the world. As it turns out, we are now officially:

We Play . . . We Score . . . A Cure for . . . ™ Foundation (Helping others is our GOAL™)

We became incorporated in 2010 and now we have trademarked our slogan ``**Playing It Forward** ™``. I hope that this charity will continue to grow long after I'm gone so it will be able to help others as it was originated to do. We have grown so much since the day we started with our dream to help others. We have helped so many people and charities and have grown our sports from ball hockey and ice hockey to include, volleyball, baseball, softball, bowling, golf, and will soon be including walks, bike rides, dinner dances and more so by the time you read this we should be adding even more events.

Visit us on our website to see where we are.

WWW.PLAYINGITFORWARD.CA

TM

JOHNNY AND NANCY BOWER

It was approximately April of 2007, when I met Johnny and Nancy Bower for the first time. I had been in contact him through a friend who was helping me build the tournament we started for Multiple Sclerosis, originally called 'We Shoot . . . We Score . . . A Cure for MS'. Johnny was an amazing person who was willing to help us out in every way possible.

Johnny would be anywhere and everywhere if he could. He seems to have this boundless energy and he is so friendly to everyone he has ever met. We had arranged for him to sign some photos and pucks and he agreed to even be at our tournament the following July. I told Johnny we would arrange his rides and all the necessary details to get him to the tournament. I remember calling my Father and asking him if he would pick someone up for the tourney. He replied yes of course. (Remember I said I would give my Dad the biggest surprise of his life?)

He asked who and where from. I told him, "Johnny Bower from the Toronto Maple Leafs.", and I swear I heard the phone hit the floor. I had just made his life's dream come true. (He loves the Leafs.) I'm so very proud I was able to make this wish come true for him as he has made so many come true for me. Thanks Dad

We worked very close with Johnny while we were planning the event and I remember him saying we should get in touch with Richard (Dickie) Duff, another legend from the

Toronto Maple Leafs. I contacted him and he was honoured to help us. So we started the planning of our first tournament for Multiple Sclerosis. My Dad was so excited that he was going to meet his hero. He washed and waxed his car until it shone. After all, he was picking up Johnny Bower! I was so glad I could give him this wonderful, totally unexpected surprise that I knew would mean so very much to him. I know what I have put him through in our lifetime together and I am so happy this opportunity came for me to put a big smile on his face.

Johnny was at our first event with us and signed autographs all day. He even coached a team as a surprise. He was amazing and has been with us ever since. He was very upset that the MS Society backed out on us and he told us he would be with us all the way.

Johnny and Nancy were with us at our fundraiser for my surgery as well and Johnny gave an emotional speech. It was very touching. We have tried to do other projects together to help others and we have also met at some other events where we didn't know each other were attending. I have one Leaf jersey which I will cherish forever. This was given to me by Johnny and Nancy themselves. It is a Bower jersey and he signed it for me.

I have become a true Johnny Bower fan (still not a Leaf fan though). Johnny and Nancy visit us quite often at our home now as it is almost impossible for me to get out and we love sharing our home with them where they know they are always welcome.

I love being able to watch an Old Timers hockey game and seeing him play, then asking questions about the game and listening while he tells me the details. I remember I was expecting them for a visit and I was watching the 1964 All Star game. Johnny was in net. Well, Johnny and Nancy came over and I told them I was watching the 1964 All Star game and he was playing and he said, "Oh yeah. We lost that game 3-2." I could only laugh as he just gave away the score. Johnny reminds me so much of my Grandfather and they look so much alike to me. He is like my Grandfather in many ways and I admire that about him. I miss my Grandparents and when I'm with Johnny and Nancy it seems like I have them here with me again. He is not just Johnny Bower the legend, He is my friend.

We have developed a great friendship that has lasted to this day. They are like family to my wife, kids and I and I love them as family. (Johnny will get the first copy of this book)

I recently won a picture of Johnny in an online hockey auction. It's funny because I can get a signed picture from him anytime but this one was very nice and I wanted it. Well I watched, I bid and **I won it**!! It is proudly displayed on my living room wall right beside my desk. I look at it every day and am reminded just how blessed I am to know him and how special he is as a friend to me. I have two things I will cherish forever. The jersey he gave me and this picture. I have a number of items, sticks, pucks, helmets and more with his signature on them but these two rank Number One and Number One in my collection. (No, that is not a typing mistake. They are in that order for me.)

Eleven Days In Hell

It was a beautiful mid May Saturday afternoon and we had invited a good friend over for a barbeque as well as to give some training lessons to our friend's son who was playing on our son's hockey team. I was always interested in and looked forward to opportunities to assist kids in their hockey skill development. I have been involved in hockey for many years and love helping kids in their pursuit of hockey and helping them learn something new each time they play the game.

The day started off very nice. The weather was hot, somewhere near thirty degrees as I remember. I had some minor discomfort in my chest but it was nothing to be concerned about (at least so I thought). I sat in the sun for quite some time and was enjoying the day when I started to feel a few odd chest pains which I just brushed off as being a sign of too much sun for me. I went into the house to cool off, parked in my chair to watch some television, grabbed a blanket and sat back for a while. I felt my feet and legs swelling which is normal for me when I'm in the heat. I had more strange chest pains and thought I may have broken another rib which was pretty common for me those days. The pain was direct but manageable so again I just thought it was the heat. Later that night I made my way up to bed as I was just not feeling well. I had my dinner and a drink but could not finish either which was unusual for me.

It was around eleven in the evening when I started having more severe chest pains and trouble breathing. I was trying to recline in my chair and couldn't seem to breathe but when I put my chair upright I found I was able to catch my breath better although not properly. I started to become very concerned, even though I thought it was a broken rib again. I tried to ignore it for about an hour and was just about to take my Tylenol's extra strength and go to sleep as these intended to make me pass out quickly but before I took them I woke up my wife and told her I wasn't able to breathe. She actually got mad at me as she had just fallen asleep, but I knew something was wrong with me and told her that. She called 911 and within minutes two ambulances, a fire truck and fire rescue were on scene at my house. This was shortly after midnight. My bedroom was instantly filled with five or six paramedics all trying to get pulse reading and heart monitors on me. It was quite an effort to get me out of the house and onto the stretcher as I was two hundred and forty pounds which is not considered to be a small size. Finally they got me down the stairs, onto the stretcher, into the ambulance, hooked up to a monitor and away we went with the sirens blaring. I didn't remember the ambulance ride or that I was in one being rushed to the hospital. I remember getting close to the hospital and saying to the paramedic, "We must be close to the hospital.", to which he asked "How do you know that?" I told him I could hear an ambulance siren and with that comment he looked at me like he was thinking, "Ahh, you dimwit. It's you in the ambulance going to the hospital." I was rushed straight into the emergency ward and had nurses and doctors coming in and out to check me over. My wife arrived shortly afterwards. The doctors told her they were going to do a number of tests and an x-ray and for her to go home. They would call her to let her know the findings. I was immediately taken to get my x-ray and then was returned to my room whereupon my nurse came in and asked me if I believed in God. I told her I was struggling with my religion and wasn't sure. She said, "I think we should pray now and pray hard." She held my hands tightly, and said a very beautiful prayer which brought tears to my eyes. She spoke quietly for about ten minutes, kissed my forehead and said, "God is now taking over." She had seen my x-rays and knew how dire my condition was but she didn't say anything to me about it. Her prayer told me more than she ever needed to.

I prayed hard the rest of the night. It was about four o'clock in the morning and I asked the doctors not to call my wife so she could continue to sleep. The doctors monitored me closely for the next few hours and then said I was going for a cat scan the next morning. The night was very long for me and the unknown was terrifying. It was Saturday when I had been brought to the hospital and I would have to wait until Monday for the CT scan.

I went for the CT scan early in the morning and had this dye put into my veins so the scan could read it. I felt this strange warm feeling winding its way through my veins and I felt like I was wetting myself. I asked the technician how things looked. He told me he couldn't say but that it did not appear pretty. I was taken back to my room where my wife was waiting for me. The Doctor came in, told us we were very close to losing me as I had a massive blood clot on my left lung the size of a golf ball and that they were very concerned about it. The Doctor spoke about a procedure that was available called a Clot Buster and spoke very seriously about this to us. He explained that if my blood pressure dropped this would have to be injected into my heart and I had one chance. It either worked or would kill me on the spot. This was my life they were talking about and I was terrified. I remember the nurse giving me a huge shot of morphine and a shot of the blood thinner at the same time. Needless to say, I had a reaction to it. I felt like I was collapsing and started to sweat. I wondered if this was going to be my moment of truth. The Doctor monitored my heart rate and blood pressure and was happy with the fact it didn't drop. I was kept in critical care and monitored until a room became available for me. The first night was unbelievable as I was in such pain. I remember lying on the emergency bed and thinking how uncomfortable it was and questioned how much longer it would be before I got into a room. I recall an unusually quiet moment and how strange that silence was. It was not to last. There had been a multiple stabbing and I don't mean one person. There were several people being rushed into the Emergency and it was chaotic. Three o'clock in the morning and I was now wide awake again. It lasted about an hour then seemed to calm down a bit. I was taken into a room at about five o'clock, still in emergency, but I now had a room to myself where I managed to get some sleep.

The doctors came in and explained what was going to be done to me during this procedure they had recommended. I remained in this room for another nine hours I think and then I was taken to a private room. I had been given private rooms for some years after they found I was susceptible to MRSA when I had my stomach surgery. At that time they had put me into a standard ward room with three other people and one of them had this illness, MRSA, so I was exposed to it. When this came to light I was immediately rushed into a private room and put under extreme watch. Everyone who came to visit me had to wear gowns and masks. I was tested for the MRSA and found to be clear of it. However, once the fact I had been exposed to it was put on my medical records in the computer I was permanently red flagged as a MRSA patient. So every time I go into a hospital I'm put into a private room and everyone is forced to wear a hospital gown when they visit me even though it is a known fact that I didn't have MRSA.

I was taken to my room and monitored every hour or half hour for three days straight. I had regular blood tests and blood thinner injections. My wife arranged for me to always have someone with me for company. On the fourth day I was moved to another room as I was now out of critical care. I was so happy that I had made it out of another near death situation in my life. I was taken to a room on the fifth floor which is Respirology and the room was the size of a closet. It may have been small but it had all the equipment that would be needed in the event something went wrong. The view of a rooftop was not so desirable though. This was the second room I had been put into with an unpleasant view but I was breathing so I wasn't complaining. I stayed in this room for three days and then we found that it had a television and radio. I wasn't sure how to work the television so I put the radio on and went to sleep for a while. After my wife left I finally got the television working and was relaxing watching it when a nurse came in to see me. She told me they may be moving me to yet another room and I told her that I had just gotten the television to work. They ultimately decided they were not moving me, so I relaxed and actually went back to sleep. Later that night a nurse came in and told me they were moving me down the hall to another room after all. I was mad at this and said "No Way! You are not moving me again." The nurse became agitated with me so she went to complain. The Administrator came in later and asked me what was wrong so I explained that I had been moved four times already, had just been able to get the television working, would not be able to get another one until the next day and I was not going to miss the hockey game which was currently on. The Administer asked if they could move me after the game ended and I told her that while I was not happy about it, if they could get the television working for me right away in the next room I would move. They wanted the room I was in because it was equipped with all the oxygen tanks and hoses that were required for the next patient. I was moved to my fifth room around eleven o'clock in the evening and was able to get settled quickly. Also, surprisingly to me, I now had a roommate as they had put me into a semi–private room which was an unusual move for me. This was all right with me though as he was very pleasant. I was awakened at six o'clock in the morning for blood work and to have my blood pressure taken. I felt like I just fallen to sleep, but it was nothing new for me as this was when they always did their rounds. A few hours later a doctor came in and told me they wanted to do a test on my thyroid as something had come up in the test results that were abnormal. I called my wife as she had to go through the same thing and she was diagnosed with Thyroid Cancer. I was freaking out and said no way I'm going to get something else on top of all I have to deal with. I was going to refuse the test as I was already in the hospital for a period of six days with no physiotherapy and I knew that not walking was going to have a very negative effect on my legs. I had been begging for therapy for days and I was given physiotherapy only once during my stay up to this point. I told my wife that I was not going to do this test as I wanted to come home and work on my legs first then worry about the test later. My wife was very angry with my decision and was going to do anything to keep me there to have the test done. She took my clothes home and would not bring my wheelchair in as she knew I was going to leave. I was told my test would be done as soon as possible and so I said fine.

A doctor came in and told me they were going to do my test at nine o'clock in the morning which was the next day so I decided to stay. The next morning nine o'clock passed and then at eleven I asked what was happening and the Doctor said they were busy with other emergencies. So I waited and then at five o'clock I again asked what was happening.

They now informed me the Doctor had gone home. I lost it. I was so angry. I asked them what was going on? I had been assured my name was on the list for the test first thing in the morning. I reluctantly agreed to wait and remember I'm lying in a bed with no physiotherapy. Finally the Doctor came in with a pill for me, told me it would put me out for the test and that it should only take ten minutes for the pill to work. After twenty-five minutes I was still wide awake, so they gave me another one and fifteen minutes later I was still awake. Finally after the fourth pill, even though I was still wide awake they decided to start the test. I told them exactly what was happening as I was not asleep. I felt every move of the needle that was in my throat and was telling the Doctor this during the test. It felt very strange but it was finally over. I thought great and was relieved I had gotten through everything. Then I passed out from all the previous medication and apparently slept for twenty-seven hours. The Doctor told me I could go home and I was to have the daily injections of Cumiden (Rat poison) which were my blood thinner and have a blood test every second day until my INR levels were between two and three which are normal levels for someone on blood thinners. Now it was time to get out of there and back home where I belonged which I did. I could barely move. My legs felt like they were dead. It took me so long to get in the van but this I don't recall as I was still so drugged up. My wife said I was so angry when I came home because I could not stand up. I was very vocal and apparently very violent tempered. I guess so. I had just spent eleven days in bed and now I wasn't able to walk at all. I was so very depressed I begged for death to come to me. I beat my legs and the doctors warned me against this as this may have been a factor in my blood clot but I did it anyway and it felt great.

I hate my legs and the pain I feel in them. I feel that this situation is not my fault and I figure if I'm going to hurt like this then it should be my fault. I have beaten them until they are bruised. I'm so angry with my life but it is my poor wife and kids who are suffering so much because of my MS. I deal with it and they are forced to hear about it. I have a nurse who comes in and gives me a needle in my stomach every day until they can take me off the needles and just have me on the pills. Now I need to learn how to walk again. I have an occupational therapist who comes in two times a week to stretch my legs and help me learn to walk again with my walker. Today I took my first steps on my own with my walker. Although it was only fifteen to twenty feet it felt like it was fifteen to twenty miles. Once again I'm on my way back up the ladder. Let's see what happens next.

One thing I did do while I was in the hospital is really think of my death. Very scary, but It was top of the list in my mind. It's funny what you do when you come so close to dying. I have made it very clear to my wife and family that I want to be cremated and kept at home with my wife. She and my sons are everything to me and I want to spend eternity with them. The one thing that scared me more than death itself was whether my wife would meet somebody else? This terrifies me to no end. I cannot imagine her with someone else. Never, ever, ever. I asked her to keep my ashes at home and to be kept with her for eternity but if she did meet someone to please throw my ashes away. I pray she will not be with anyone in any way. I have told her the same for myself if, God forbid, something happened to her. I married her for eternity. I will never remarry or be with anyone else for any reason for the rest of my life. That is my promise to her. I cannot imagine my poor kids calling someone else Dad or having someone else at their wedding, graduations and special moments in their lives where I should be.

·THYROID CANCER

Back when I was in the hospital I had a biopsy on my throat, as you may remember, to check my thyroid. Well guess what? Another hurdle to try to get over, I was diagnosed with Thyroid Cancer on Tuesday, June 14, 2011. Now I must have another surgery and they will remove my thyroid. I must come off my blood thinners and do the surgery and then restart my blood thinners again to get my levels right. So many problems and no solutions in sight it seems. I hate needles and now must get more and more and more. My stomach looks like a pin cushion and is black and blue from the needles I'm taking for my blood levels.

So now I'm battling depression and dealing with all this. It is very hard. I have begged God to give me a miracle to be able to be here for my family. With this going on and no end in sight, how can I not question my religion?

I decided what I would do now is keep a journal of sorts of my daily activities until my surgery. A different twist to the book but I'm very scared of this surgery, the outcome and want to share my feelings, thoughts and updates as I go through this battle. This is what this book is about. Helping me cope with all that is going on, helping me understand the where, why, what, when and how did I get so sick and to possibly help others while they may be going through some tough times in their lives.

I must always thank my wife for her incredible strength through this as she has also had to deal with all of this plus dealing with the everyday running of our household, the kids, bills, shopping, work and everything else. If you think I'm strong you need to meet my wife.

MY DAILY LOG:

Tuesday, June 14, 2011.

9:30 am my wife and I go into the Doctor's office and he says, "Let me shut the door." I instantly think this is a bad sign. He explains that they found something in the biopsy that they didn't like. They called it suspicious. You usually know when they say suspicious you know that it means bad flat out. He said I really don't like the look of this and with that I was diagnosed with Thyroid Cancer. I saw the same

Doctor that sees my wife as, yes, she had this as well. It is very rare that two people that are married get something like this. It is not contagious in anyway, but I asked just in case. I almost broke down right there but I always feel I need to be strong for my wife as she is so strong for me. I use her strength to help me to get through things every day.

I came home and sat by myself and truly thought about what is going to happen. I went into a deep dark place of depression, I cried by myself for a while as I was terrified that I won't be there for my kids' weddings, graduations or any others meaningful events in their lives. My body is overwhelmed and aching like crazy. I have not had a sore throat for ten years and funny now my throat is bugging me. I wonder if this is the placebo effect?

Wednesday, June 15, 2011.

My thoughts today are to try to deal with this one day at a time and to do the surgery and pray hard. I was questioning doing the surgery but the Doctor said it would be a very dangerous move as the cancer would spread to my throat, brain and eventually kill me. I tried to relax and not to let it bother me so much but I'm still so terrified of this surgery. My day was basically uneventful but still full of questions about the surgery. I ask myself, "What if? What if?" It seems to be a constant question that I guess everyone goes through when they are so confused, scared, and feeling helpless. I waited for the hockey game to come on in the evening as it seems that hockey takes me away to a different place, to worry about nothing else but trying to get the players to hear me yelling at them to move the puck or make a play. It was an exciting night, game seven of the NHL playoffs so I watched the Boston Bruins win the Stanley cup, but unfortunately what was on my mind was the surgery and will I make it through it. Even though it was the biggest game of the year I was stressing over my situation. It is a seemingly basic surgery these days but with MS, Colitis, the lung and all the other stuff I have to deal with it will be so much more challenging.

I actually cried again watching my wife sleep as I want to be here for her and our boys every day. They are truly what keep me going. I sometimes just watch her sleep and just try to relax as she is so peaceful while she is far away and dreaming. It seems to relax me a bit. I say quietly, "I love you.", and go to sleep myself.

Thursday, June 16, 2011.

I wake up today feeling a bit better about what is soon to come. Not sure if it is acceptance or just trying to focus on something else.

My sister has found peace in her life as she is going through some stuff and wants to share it with me. I'm quite sceptical about this but must keep an open mind. I have tried to pray to God unsuccessfully for years so maybe this may work for me. I have said it before. Give me something to believe in because this God thing isn't working out so well.

Today is a physiotherapy day so I'm looking forward to having it as that is a real release of all that troubles me for the half hour I do it. I stretch my legs to the point they ache but again it seems like I drift to a different place, a good place. It is similar to going to a gym and saying, "Man, that was a hell of a workout and I feel great."

Friday, June 16, 2011.

I woke up feeling very depressed and confused about what is going to happen with the surgery and whether I should do it or not. I spoke to my wife and understandably she is truly annoyed that I even think this way. I have made a decision and I'm going to stick to it.

In the evening we have a number of friends come over and we discuss it with them to mixed reviews. I say I'm not going to go through with the surgery because I'm afraid of being on the blood thinners as there may be a chance I bleed to death while doing surgery and without blood thinners my clot may come back and I would die anyway. I'm alive right now and may just stay with this plan until further notice. Our friends have their opinions and I love to hear both sides so to speak. I feel mixed emotions but will have a second opinion done to clear my mind. But for now—NO SURGERY.

Saturday, June, 18, 2011.

Today we have my family all coming over for a barbeque for my Mom's birthday. The day goes well. We start off with my middle child's hockey game. I coach his team, sometimes from the bench and sometimes from the stands. So today it was from the stands as I cannot get my wheelchair to the bench. I was told not go get stressed out as this could have a major effect of my clot, but no, not me I don't listen and I get caught up in the moment and boy did I pay for it. I had trouble breathing and was quite concerned but it is hockey and we won. So into the playoffs we go. Saturday afternoon my family comes and we have a wonderful afternoon and I explain my decision to them. They each have mixed feelings as can well be expected. I said I just came out from eleven days of hell and no physiotherapy which I was supposed to get and I have this blood clot that nearly killed me. I just want to get this sorted out before I do anything else. Most agreed.

Sunday, June 19, 2011.

Today we have another hockey game at one o'clock and it is Father's Day, so we plan to go out for lunch. The day starts off great and we go to our son's hockey game. They have to win or they are eliminated, so I tell them it is all or nothing, we have to win it. We're playing for the championship. If we lose we go home and watch television all summer and I hate television. The game is stressful as the other team's coach has the kids falling on every bump, stick or collision, faking hurts and diving like they are in a pool. I'm so angry, that when I see this disgusting display of sportsmanship I want our kids to win even more. I keep yelling to the referees to pay attention as they seem like complete fools who barley know the game let alone know how to referee. We tie the game and go into overtime and I usually go down to the dressing room when there is one minute left in the game, but I'm not going anywhere during overtime. Overtime finishes and now we go to a shootout. I'm glued to my chair as this is it, all or nothing. My son is the first shooter. Down the ice he goes, shoots and a very nice save by their goalie. We go to the third shooter as no one has scored and he goes down the ice towards the net, shoots, SCORES and we win. We are going to the championship game. I'm freaking out I'm so excited, so I head down to the dressing room and doesn't the elevator get stuck! I need to be down there with my kids and the elevator doesn't work. I lose my mind I'm so angry. My wife makes a comment that I take as mocking me and I lash out at her. I never meant to but it was the heat of the moment and I felt we should be downstairs, not stuck at an elevator. I waited for what seemed like forever and finally got it to come upstairs. By the time I got down some of my kids were already gone.

I congratulated them on a great game and thanked them for not acting like the other team. We played as a team and won as a team. Fair and square.

We did not go out for Father's Day as my wife was angry at me. I said I was sorry and I meant it.

Monday, June, 20, 2011.

Today is a normal day. I have physiotherapy and exercise with a new nurse. I was able to sleep last night and today am looking forward to trying to walk. I walk about forty feet with my nurse following me with a chair. I made it so I'm very happy. Not really thinking of this whole surgery thing today.

Tuesday, June, 21, 2011.

Today is a boring day, didn't walk as I had a wound nurse here for my stomach to check it out to make sure all was okay. Did some stretching of my legs so they don't seize but not much happening. Happy Birthday Mom.

Skip a few boring days.

Thursday, June 23, 2011

I had my youngest son's Junior Kindergarten graduation today. It was so sweet to see him get his diploma. He didn't sing but that's all right. We had a desert table set up as the parents all brought something in for treats after. My son went up and got two plates and put them on my lap. The other parents said, "Oh, how sweet.", because he got cookies, cakes, strawberries, cup cakes and split them all up between the two plates. I went to take a cookie from one plate and he said, "No that's mine.", so I reached for a treat from the other plate and he said, "No that's mine too." How sweet? He was hoarding so the others didn't take everything and he wouldn't even share his goodies with me. Ha! Ha! That was so funny and the other parents were laughing as well.

Friday, June 24, 2011.

A regular, boring day in most cases but we did have a family get together which I love when we do it at our house. I'm not able to go to others houses as they are not accessible for me. We had a great time and my cousin also came over for visit. We stayed up until about two-thirty in the morning.

Sunday, June 26, 2011.

We had our son's ball hockey championship game. I was very excited that they made it this far as his team has had some challenges. He has worked very hard and has been noticed for his efforts. He will be playing in the 'A' Elite Division next year. They lost 5-2 but my son got two points, so another strong game for him. I'm so proud of him.

Now what to do?

Friday, July 1, 2011.

My wife had been planning our annual street barbeque that is always held on the July 1st long weekend. It is always such great fun. A chance to forget the problems of everyday and just eat, drink and mingle with our neighbours. We bought a small blow up pool for the kiddies to play in but it turned out to be a water trap for most who walked by it. People were getting pushed in and so began the water fight part of the day. Water balloons, buckets and the hose. We had an amazing fireworks display to wind down the evening and finally closed up at around two o'clock in the morning. We thoroughly enjoyed our day. The annual 'Hemlark Court BBQ' was a great success.

ONE, TWO, SKIP A FEW DAYS . . .

Wednesday, July 13, 2011.

I saw my surgeon today and the news is that my thyroid must come out. I was not going to go through with the surgery but it seems that I don't get a second chance with this so it is booked for September 26, 2011 (which coincidently is our 19th wedding anniversary). I asked all the questions I could think of to get out of it. I asked about the blood thinners which will be a problem and I will have to go off them, then back on again with all the needles until my levels are normal again. I also asked for physiotherapy this time as I did not get it last time. My wife said she is not ready to lose me yet and that really sunk in. I would give the world for my wife and kids, so I guess giving up my thyroid is part of it.

So here go the fears, questions, concerns, thoughts, prayers and all that comes with another surgery.

I'm constantly battling the thoughts of not doing the surgery and just taking my chances. I feel I may have a longer life just not doing the surgery. I don't want to constantly be bothered by the surgery and the after effects that I may face.

I want to work hard at trying to walk a bit and stay strong for my fight against Multiple Sclerosis.

I need to stay on the blood thinners for life and need to focus on the clot until it diminishes completely.

Well, I decided to bite the bullet and do the surgery after all.

Monday, September 26, 2011.

This was a cold day and was the day I was to have my surgery to remove my thyroid. Did I mention it was my 19th WEDDING ANNIVERSARY? I was so scared something would go wrong and I would never see my beautiful wife and fabulous kids again. I was constantly grabbing her hand and telling her how much I love her. I always tell her I love her, but I wanted to ensure my last words if they were going to be would be. I LOVE YOU and THANK YOU. We checked in at nine in the morning and my surgery was booked for noon so we had time to sit and talk and just reflect. I told my wife if something happened I wanted some of my memorabilia to be given away to very special people and that I wanted to be cremated and brought home to be with her and the boys.

I was prepped and ready to go. Noon came slowly and went by and my surgery was delayed, so the anxiety started again. Finally at about twelve-fifty pm the call came in. It was time. I had tears in my eyes watching my wife drift away as I was thinking about her and our boys. I remember being in the operating room and asking the nurse, "Please bring me home?" That was the last I remember. I woke up in the ICU unit as if nothing happened but felt like someone had hit me in the throat with a sledge hammer.

I had my whole thyroid removed along with eight of ten lymph nodes. They did put back my parathyroid gland. To give a bit of information on the thyroid:

In <u>vertebrate</u> <u>anatomy</u>, the **thyroid gland** or simply, the **thyroid** (), is one of the largest <u>endocrine glands</u>. The thyroid gland is found in the <u>neck</u>, below (<u>inferior</u> to) the <u>thyroid cartilage</u> (which forms the <u>laryngeal prominence</u>, or 'Adam's Apple'). The isthmus (the bridge between the two lobes of the thyroid) is located inferior to the <u>cricoid cartilage</u>.

The thyroid gland controls how quickly the body uses energy, makes <u>proteins</u>, and controls how sensitive the body should be to other <u>hormones</u>. It participates in these processes by producing thyroid hormones, the principal ones being <u>triiodothyronine</u> (T_3) and <u>thyroxine</u> (T_4). These hormones regulate the rate of metabolism and affect the growth and rate of function of many other systems in the body. T_3 and T_4 are synthesized from both iodine and tyrosine. The thyroid also produces calcitonin, which plays a role in calcium homeostasis.

Hormonal output from the thyroid is regulated by thyroid-stimulating hormone (TSH) produced by the anterior pituitary, which itself is regulated by thyrotropin-releasing hormone (TRH) produced by the hypothalamus.

The thyroid gets its name from the Greek word for "shield", after the shape of the related thyroid cartilage. The most common problems of the thyroid gland consist of an overactive thyroid gland, referred to as hyperthyroidism, and an underactive thyroid gland, referred to as hypothyroidism.

The Parathyroid gland works like this:

The **parathyroid glands** are small endocrine glands in the neck that produce parathyroid hormone. Humans usually have four parathyroid glands, which are usually located on the rear surface of the thyroid gland, or, in rare cases, within the thyroid gland itself or in the chest. Parathyroid glands control the amount of calcium in the blood and within the bones.

All went well and my throat seems to be healing nicely. Cross my fingers.

I received the call from the Doctor's office that I could never have imagined. My thyroid contained cancer and three of the eight lymph nodes also contained cancer, so I'm glad they got it out. Imagine that. And it was found by accident.

I hope they got it all as they are not going back in. My body can't handle anymore.

Depression Is Killing Me

 have been battling a depression for many years and I guess it was finally recognized.

Depression is defined as:

Depression may be described as feeling sad, blue, unhappy, miserable, or down in the dumps. Most of us feel this way at one time or another for short periods.

True clinical depression is a mood disorder in which feelings of sadness, loss, anger, or frustration interfere with everyday life for weeks or longer.

Causes, incidence, and risk factors

The exact cause of depression is not known. Many researchers believe it is caused by chemical changes in the brain. This may be due to a problem with your genes, or triggered by certain stressful events. More likely, it's a combination of both.

Some types of depression run in families. But depression can also occur if you have no family history of the illness. Anyone can develop depression, even kids.

The following may play a role in depression:

- Alcohol or drug abuse
- Certain medical conditions, including underactive thyroid, cancer, or long-term pain
- Certain medications such as steroids
- Sleeping problems
- Stressful life events, such as:
    - Breaking up with a boyfriend or girlfriend
    - Failing a class
    - Death or illness of someone close to you
- Divorce
    - Childhood abuse or neglect
    - Job loss
    - Social isolation (common in the elderly)

Symptoms

Depression can change or distort the way you see yourself, your life, and those around you.

People who have depression usually see everything with a more negative attitude, unable to imagine that any problem or situation can be solved in a positive way.

Symptoms of depression can include:

- Agitation, restlessness, and irritability
- Dramatic change in appetite, often with weight gain or loss
- Very difficult to concentrate
- Fatigue and lack of energy
- Feelings of hopelessness and helplessness
- Feelings of worthlessness, self-hate, and guilt
- Becoming withdrawn or isolated
- Loss of interest or pleasure in activities that were once enjoyed
- Thoughts of death or suicide
- Trouble sleeping or excessive sleeping

Depression can appear as anger and discouragement, rather than feelings of sadness.

If depression is very severe, there may also be psychotic symptoms, such as hallucinations and delusions.

Signs and tests

Your health care provider will ask questions about your medical history and symptoms. Your answers and certain questionairres can help your doctor make a diagnosis of depression and determine how severe it may be.

Blood and urine tests may be done to rule out other medical conditions with symptoms similar to depression.

Treatment

In general, treatments for depression include:

- Medications called antidepressants
- Talk therapy, called psychotherapy

If you have mild depression, you may only need one of these treatments. People with more severe depression usually need combination of both treatments. It takes time to feel better, but there are usually day-to-day improvements.

If you are suicidal or extremely depressed and cannot function you may need to be treated in a psychiatric hospital.

> But please get the help that you need. It is very important.

I have been building up a feeling inside of worthlessness like crazy. I feel like I'm a burden to my family and constantly think they would be better off without me. I have had all the symptoms of depression listed above but none of the stressful life events listed above. My stress is Multiple Sclerosis, Cancer, Colitis, blood clots and constant pain.

There is a constant feeling of almost anger when I wake up. I think to myself, "Is this going to be a good day or another one full of pain and anxiety?" I sit alone all day and drive myself insane with the thoughts of whether I will ever walk again or will my body stop working today. My body constantly cramps and goes into seizures about a hundred times a day. My physiotherapist calls this severe spasticity whereas I call it damn painful and irritating. My body stretches out to a straight position constantly or cramps and my legs bend back up like I'm going into the fetal position and the pain is so intense. My hands cramp so much I can't hold a pen or pencil. My feet burn like I'm walking on red hot coals and the tingling going through my body feels like I'm licking a nine volt battery or being constantly electrocuted.

I have lost the relationship my wife and I once had. We have seemingly drifted apart. I love her more than anything but there seems to be miles between us now. And it is the medical circumstances and the constant dealing with it that has created this daily lifestyle which cannot help but affect our relationship. I sleep in a chair and she sleeps in our bed. I want to snuggle or hold her or have intimate time whereas she is so exhausted from managing everything including me that she needs her sleep to be able to cope with the next day because she is so mentally, emotionally and physically exhausted from the daily burdens and responsibilities that have been placed on her. MS has taken that part away from me too as well for the most part because as they say if you don't use it you lose it. I feel neglected, rejected and dejected and every 'ed' you can think of. 'ED' is killing me. I have even asked her for a piece of her clothing to sleep with so I can smell her scent because I want to feel close to her through the night.

I get angry very quickly as I just want the house to run smoothly for my wife. Little things drive me crazy. I want my wife and I to have us time as well because I truly don't know if I will be here the next day. I'm so scared of leaving her as a widow at such a young age and I am especially anxious about the children. I don't want to leave them fatherless. I am so anxious about that thought. I want to see them graduate so badly but I don't feel my body will let me live that long. I became ill with the MS and thought I could beat it. Then Colitis decides it will try to stop me, so I had to stress my body to fight them both at the same time. Then I get the blood clot and really start to panic that now I have to fight three things and then just to top it off along comes Thyroid Cancer. "What did I do to deserve all this?" I ask myself that question time and time again. "Why does my family have to suffer so much? Would it be easier if I wasn't here?" This is where the depression is getting me. It is the unknown that hurts so much! Why does it feel so horrible? I feel miserable all the time especially when I can't go somewhere with my family. It is the lowest of low feelings in the world. I feel like I'm a stone that's been thrown into the water and I'm just becoming a big ripple effect slowly but steadily diminishing into the current. Vanishing.

I sit alone and constantly think how much longer I have. I always have, and will always tell my wife how much I love her every day and to tell her how beautiful she is. I say I never want to die tomorrow without telling her and our boys every day how thankful I am to them for their love and support.

My wife and boys mean everything to me and I want to spend all my time with them. I think this is my only part, that desire, that fights the depression. My family is the most important thing to me and I would do anything for them.

My wife holds me when I cry and when I hurt and when I need help. I just hate the feeling of sitting in a chair and her outside with the kids and I can't do anything at all to be a part of the family. I ask, "Do they miss me?", when they are enjoying themselves without me?

I understand that they must do things with the family, but I wish they would remember how lonely I will be when they are gone. There is a lot of pain behind this smile. It hurts so much to sit alone.

I asked Santa for legs or death for Christmas. Not a position a father or husband should ever be in. Depression is just killing me.

I was diagnosed as the most positive depressed person my therapist has met. I battle all this and yet still strive to help others in any way possible. (This is my medication for depression.)

*Everybody is different and again make sure to ask lots of questions and have faith in your body and mind that you will make the right decision for yourself. Knowledge is power.

I had often thought of writing a letter to my disease, but thought it was kind of corny. I decided to write it and see how I felt afterwards.

I write this as a therapeutic release and way to truly vent my anger and frustration. Try it, it really works. No one has to know, it is yours to do what you want with it. Whether it is a disease, illness, a condition or a problem you are dealing with. Let it know how you feel. How you truly feel.

DEAR DISEASE

(A Letter From Me)

I know I will not get an answer or even a reply from you, and this is a very hard thing to get a grasp of, knowing that I will never get a definitive answer but I must express my anger and hatred towards you. I ask myself everyday **WHY?** Why did I get you for life? What did I do to deserve you? This is something you would ask of a love or a wife, not something that is so horrible, so painful and so downright destructive. I don't hate many things but I can swear to you with all that is holy **I HATE YOU!! I hate you** for what you have done to me, my family and my life. You have destroyed a husband, a father, a son and a brother and for this **I hate you.** You have taken my legs, my arms, my body, my mind, my heart and my soul and for this **I hate you.** You have taken away my sports and my ability to share all these with my kids (my poor kids). How do I explain to them I can't play as my body hurts so much I can't bear it and for this **I hate you.** I wake up disgusted that I woke up and wonder what my day will hold and for this **I hate you.** The depression that is ripping apart a very friendly outgoing person is horrible and for this **I hate you.**

I cry, I scream, I beat myself regularly, I have violent convulsions, I fall, I cramp so bad you can't even imagine (but I guess you do know this and just don't care) and for this **I hate you.** You are the worst thing I could imagine happening to such a great family. How dare you take me away from my kids. What gives you the right? My innocent five year old child asked Santa for legs for his Daddy for Christmas and was so very disappointed when I didn't get them and for this **I hate you.** You have made me struggle with my religion, my faith and trust in God, my wanting to live, my ability to just be me and for this **I hate you.**

You have given me many slaps in the face yet, through all your adversity you have also given rise to my incredible passion to help other disabled people and to assist them in their ongoing fight like I could never have imagined. My charity foundation and my ability to write this book also came to fruition because of you. You have caused me to meet some great people, actually I should say amazing life changing people that are changing the world for the better and who have inspired me to set my sights on the same goal-making a difference.

You have made me see just how incredibly strong my wife and family are. You have made me appreciate just how much they do for me and how much I need them. I love my wife so much for her perpetual strength, patience and compassion all the while knowing I'm steadily going downhill and that I'm eventually going to be bedridden. I love, admire, and honour my boys for their unquestionable strength in coping with your injustice and disruption in their young lives and for still being the best loving support they can be for me while also witnessing your daily invasion of their father's body.

Yes, **MS**, you are a debilitating, unforgiving, unfair and relentless disease. But from you and through you my family and I have joined forces and have learned that what **MS** truly means is **MORE STRENGTH** and for this **I forgive you.**

MANY IN MOTION

On November 7, 2011 I received a call that will truly change my life forever. I had applied to be a part of the Rick Hansen Man in Motion 25th Anniversary Tour across Canada and to carry the medal in my area. I have been inspired by Rick for many years and truly wanted to be a part of this amazing event.

To my surprise and amazement I was to be a part of this wonderful event. For those of you who don't know who Rick Hansen is, Rick Hansen was the gentleman who, in his wheelchair, crossed Canada in 1985 at the age of twenty-seven. Rick Hansen set out on a journey that would make history. Inspired by the dream of creating an accessible and inclusive world, and fueled by a deep seated belief that 'anything is possible', Rick and his team battled the elements and the odds for more than two years through thirty-four countries on four continents.

He wheeled the equivalent of two marathons every day (40,000 kilometres in total) before returning home to a hero's welcome in Vancouver. His Man in Motion World Tour was complete. Rick and his team had not only raised awareness of the potential of people with disabilities but they had also managed to raise Twenty-six Million Dollars to help realize Rick's dream of a truly accessible and inclusive world.

Rick was injured in 1973 after being thrown from the back of a pickup truck coming home from a fishing trip. He has since changed the world and the lives of thousands including myself.

I remember very clearly when he was doing his tour across Canada. I said, "Wow! This guy is crossing Canada in a wheelchair. That is amazing!" I was walking, playing hockey and loving life as an able bodied person, but I still felt so proud of him. Here I am twenty-five years later and I'm in a wheelchair and Rick Hansen is my hero. I looked up to him then and I idolize him now. I got the call and started to cry. I was going to be a part of the Rick Hansen 25th Anniversary Many in Motion Tour across Canada. We all met at the event location and exchanged our personal stories of what has happened to us and why we wanted to participate in this amazing venture. It was so inspiring and emotional. I cried a number of times hearing the stories of my fellow medal carriers on my leg of the event. One that inspired me the most is a fellow who had that morning returned from running in the New York City marathon. He ran eighteen miles and he is blind. The one major thing that inspires me is my wife and I have said it so many times before. She is two wings shy of being an angel. I asked her to meet me where my leg of the event started as I had a special surprise for her. I arranged this with the event co-ordinators and was the first ever to request to have my wife sit on my lap in my wheelchair and we shared the moment together. People cried when they heard my request. I met my wife at my starting spot with the police, all the flashing lights, music and total energy where I asked her to sit in my lap as this was our special time. I cried the whole way knowing that I was part of history and I got to share it with my wife. What an honour.

I was given a replica medal of the one I carried and will cherish it forever.

The Rick Hansen 25th Anniversary Relay will travel through more than 600 communities as it makes its nine-month, 12,000-kilometre journey across Canada before concluding in Vancouver on May 22, 2012 and include 7000 medal carrying participants and I was one of them.

My day was so full of inspiration and emotion I actually forgot about my pain for a day. I say a heartfelt, warmest thank you to the Rick Hansen Foundation for giving me the honour and pleasure of being a part of this truly amazing and historic event. I will remember and cherish it forever.

I was recently on a television show doing an interview regarding what Rick Hansen has meant to me now and before my disability. What an honor that was for me. See my interview below.

http://www.youtube.com/watch?v=0Wcvf1kiKjQ

Fr more on the Rick Hansen foundation please visit his website at www.RickHansen.com

HELLO GOD! IT'S ME, MARK!

have struggled with religion all my life, not certain whether something exists or not.

I was raised without religion or an understanding of one. My Grandmother was always reading her bible and going to church when she could and trying to give me some idea of religion. She would give me bibles as stocking stuffers at Christmas and I would always just put them away. She would ask me to go to Sunday school and I would say I'm busy. She was always trying to make me understand and I was just a punk kid who didn't want to listen. (It's too bad as I missed out on a lot.)

I think the first sign of religion or what was religion or would have been religion to me was when my Grandfather passed away, which was just prior to my wedding in 1992. I wondered if there was something else out there, something higher or something to look forward to after death. I didn't fully understand it and wasn't sure if I wanted to. Something just seemed to call out to me somehow. This would be something I would struggle with for many years after my Grandfather passed away. Since I became Catholic a few years ago I have been very comfortable with my thoughts of religion until recently. Do I have the 'out of sight—out of mind'syndrome I talk about? By not being in church am I forgetting my religion?

I have always felt a calm when I'm in church but real distant when I'm not. I'm going through a real bad stage right now and blame God for everything. I ask why? Why? Why? Why me? What did I do? Why do you have to make it hurt so badly? I dream I'm walking, playing with my kids and playing hockey when I'm sleeping and when I wake up it is like I'm in hell all over again. Life is miserable for me and I'm blaming God. I'm losing all hope and I'm blaming God. I say, "Hello God, it's me, Mark. Can you guide me today? Can you give me strength? Can you walk beside me through my day? Can you make the pain go away?" Then I go to move and my body cramps so badly and goes into violent convulsions and I say, "Hello God! Did you forget about me?" Am I being selfish or am I forgetting that as everyone always says, "There is always someone worse off then you." Well, I honestly don't think so at this moment.

I'm sure there are many people worse off than me and I'm sure they all say, "Hello God! Did you forget about me?"

I'm so angry with my life and the way it has become. I blame God for it all. I ask, "Who would do this to someone? If He is so powerful why would He do this? Why does He make it hurt so bad and for so long." Every day it just seems to get worse and I don't see an end in sight. I think these are questions many people ask on a regular basis and we just don't seem to know the correct answer, or any answer for that matter. I feel misguided and let down by my beliefs. I tell my wife I will never believe but then I ask for help from Him. I think my depression is playing a major part in my struggles with religion. There is a saying, 'Life is like a box of assorted chocolates, you never know what you'll get.' Well I know. I got the expired one. So for this I say, "Hello God. It's me, Mark." I have even stooped to levels so low that I have said if the devil can grant me a day without pain he can have my soul, but I guess he doesn't exist as I'm still hurting.

I think we all believe God can grant us the material things we all want and desire and this is why when we don't get our way we say, "Hello God! Remember me?" I do it all the time. I urgently need assistance remodelling my house and I ask for God's help like he is the contractor. Maybe I should ask for more guidance and peace of mind and not necessarily an extension on my home.

I'm so confused about my religion and I confuse my wife regularly about it as well. One minute I ask for help and one minute I say I don't believe. I'm not sure I don't believe, I'm sure I'm so frustrated it's hard to believe. So again I say, "Hello God! It's me, Mark."

I honestly feel everyone with a disability or illness has questioned their faith at one time or another and I believe this may make it stronger in some way. I truly struggle but when I get myself up off my wheelchair and make my transfer I thank God for his help.

If I was to write a letter to God, I think it would go something like this:

Dear God

Hello it's me, Mark. Remember me?

I wish I had the answers to life but I truly don't even know what the question is. I try so hard to be happy and helpful for everyone and I struggle to do this with my own family and life. I put up a strong front when in fact I'm falling apart. I'm the man and I'm the mouse, I'm torn apart inside and supposed to be of sound mind to endure my daily activities.

I ask you, God, "What is it you want from me? What is it I need to do? What is your goal for me? What is my future? What is my legacy? Do I fall off the face of the earth, or do I make a difference? Is there a light at the end of my tunnel? Am I one of your children or am I forgotten? Why did this happen? Why do I feel so lost?"

I feel very alone as I sit by myself with my windows and blinds closed as I don't want anyone or the world to see me this way. There is a lot of pain behind this smile. Why? I'm not a bad person. I think I have lots to offer.

I don't mean to be angry with You, I just need to vent and I guess blame something or someone and You're my closest target. I'm sorry for this. My life is a mixed up mess and the only thing that keeps me grounded is my family. I struggle with my own mind and thoughts regularly and I'm in a very dark place in my life both physically and emotionally right now.

Life seems like a game that I'm losing like it is the bottom of the ninth and I'm never going to win. This life hasn't turned out quite the way I wanted it to be. I'm searching hard for my inner peace. Help me find it so I can continue to try to be there for my family.

I ask this in Your name.

Amen

I hope He gets this letter and may bless me with some relief someday, someway, somehow.

OUT OF SIGHT, OUT OF MIND SYNDROME

You may remember back in May, 2011 I was hospitalized with what was diagnosed as a massive blood clot on my lung near my heart. This nearly took my life but I pulled through somehow and it's seems kind of funny but I was not scared of dying. Another wall was put up in front of me and again I knocked it down somewhat, or did I?

I often think of the '**out of sight, out of mind**' syndrome and it truly exists. I believe I made this fictitious ailment up but it must truly be real as it happens every day somewhere. We are a society that thinks someone else will do it or it will get better eventually somehow.

Every day we hear of people hurting, dying and/ or suffering and we usually just change the channel or have some excuse why it will be better later. I know I do it as well. I say, "Why me? Why me?" I know there are so many others worse off than me, but again 'out of sight, out of mind'. And I pray to get better, but blame the same God I'm praying to, to help me. I think we are all guilty of this at some time. We need to make changes so no one is forgotten or ignored. (Sorry, I just got side tracked a bit.)

I remember my Mom had come down in the evening to see me while I was still in emergency. It's funny how you feel being a grown man and when you see your Mom there you feel like that little child again after scrapping your knee in the park and Mom fixes it up for you. I wasn't really nervous about what was happening but I felt a reassurance while she was there. I also feel this same reassured feeling while my wife is around. I don't ask for Mom when I'm not feeling well or have hurt myself or even with what almost killed me this time.

My Mom wasn't able to come back to the hospital. I was not sure why but I took it as indicating she was just either busy or afraid of what was happening which was understandable. I was in critical care for four days and in hospital for eleven.

While I was in the hospital and after a CT scan I was also diagnosed with Thyroid Cancer and this threw me for a complete loop. Man, I could not catch a break to save my life. After being released from the hospital I was put on blood thinners for the blood clot and constantly had to have daily injections for a while to ensure the blood was flowing properly and to monitor my INR levels (International Normalized Ratio) to make sure no new blood clots appeared. We started the process regarding the Thyroid Cancer and what we needed to do and booked the date to do thyroid surgery. Coincidentally it was on my wedding anniversary, September 26th. I had not heard from my Mom since being released from the hospital for either my anniversary or for the surgery to wish me luck. I know everyone was informed for sure but I told myself it was all right not hearing from my Mom.

My guess was she may have been afraid again of talking about it or seeing me. I thought of it as a '**sweeping it under the carpet' or the 'out of sight out of mind'** syndrome as I called it. I'm always aware of it and can imagine what it is like on the other side of the proverbial fence. I thought if she didn't have the time to see me or hear about what I was going through then it was okay but, in actual truth, it really was far from okay with me.

I had the surgery on my anniversary and I was again in for the long haul. My Mom had called me while I was in the hospital and it was nice to hear her voice but it would have been so much better to see her.

I do know this for sure, if one of my kids was hospitalized I would be there every day all day no matter what. I came home and no call or visit or message whatsoever from her. I struggled through a brutal depression and anger with my illness, health problems and what my future holds and still do every day without discussing it with her.

My Dad had asked her to come for a visit in mid November. I'm still not sure if she knows that it was confirmed that it was cancer in my thyroid and lymph nodes and that I could have died from it were it not for Arlette pushing me so hard to have the surgery. It was a nice visit from her but I felt very awkward. It was like having a visit from an old friend and you don't know what to say. I asked her where she had been. There was no definitive answer. It did, however, turn out to be a very pleasant visit while it lasted.

I had recently read about the guilty feeling side of things as well. Some people feel so guilty that their kid is sick that they try to forget about it in any way they can. Maybe this can explain the **'out of sight, out of mind'** syndrome I was talking about. I say, "Don't feel guilty. It could have been something else that made me different, but I do deserve the love and support of my family like anyone else would want no matter what ailment they have, or don't have."

I have learned I really don't know how to act around someone with an ailment or disability either. How am I supposed to expect others to know what to say or to have the answers about how to act or talk to me. My guess is the '**sweep it under the carpet'** or '**out of sight, out of mind'** syndrome' really does exist and I have it also, as I truly believe I will get better someday. I'm angry, hateful, frustrated, annoyed, resentful and disrespectful to people because of this disease but I have the biggest heart and would give you the shirt off my back in the middle of winter to keep you warm if you needed it, even if it was the only one I owned. And you wouldn't even need to ask me for it.

This, I stress, is not a chapter to make anyone angry or feel hurt. It is just for my reflection and understanding about what happens through disability or illness and is it possible that the '**out of sight, out of mind'** syndrome truly exists. This is a reflection of my life and what has happened to me so many times over and over again. I have had to make many changes so others would not have reprisals or be thought of in a bad way, but for me it is my life and how I feel. Good or bad, happy or sad, it is who I am and who I've become.

I hear that some people are afraid of the unknown and when it comes to dealing with a disability it is very hard for them to cope with it. But please understand the more you forget about it the more it hurts us. **We are still here hurting, suffering, crying, and dealing with the pain.** A simple phone call does so much to make someone smile and feel cared for. Trust me.

Life's Been Good To Me So Far

Life has been a strange roller coaster for me since a very young age and it is what I have done with it that makes me so proud. I married the greatest woman of all time, I have three wonderful boys and I have been able to live in Europe and across Canada and have seen some great things. I have been able to help others deal with disabilities and illness and I have just been through so many positive experiences. I thank my wife for being there every day and tell her how much I love her and how beautiful she is daily as there will be as day I can't and I never want to go out without telling her how much I love her and our boys.

I have had ups and downs as you now know and been beaten down a number of times. I have been through some horrific car accidents, broken bones, participated in drugs, had my share of alcohol, depression, medical problems most can't handle and have done some crazy things in my life, some good, some bad and some which failed miserably but I still try to smile from time to time and say life's been good to me so far.

This has been a book for me to explore my life and to answer questions about myself. It is in no way a guide for anyone else on how to deal with or treat Multiple Sclerosis, Cancer, Depression, Colitis or other ailments. I am not a Doctor. You must trust your own instincts and ask many questions. What has worked or not worked for me may or may not work for you. We are all individuals and must listen to our own bodies, intuition, instincts, hearts, and the medical profession.

Best of luck and God Bless.

Multiple Sclerosis is a very complicated disease and we are not sure why. If you have a question, ask it and if you have an answer please share it with us. One thing I have learned about Multiple Sclerosis is we are all looking for good advice so why can't we share what we know with others? You may think you are not popular anymore but when you are diagnosed with Multiple Sclerosis you have just become a part of a family of over 75,000 people and growing every day. **NOW THAT'S POPULAR.** So let's help each other because God knows we are going to need it.

One thing I like to do when I talk to one person or a group of people is to ask the question: *"**Do you know somebody with Multiple Sclerosis**?"* If they say no, I shake their hand, introduce myself and say, "Now you have a friend with Multiple Sclerosis."

It sort of melts the proverbial ice.

I will talk to anyone with Multiple Sclerosis or illness if they need me. Anyone can contact me ANYTIME at weplaywescore@rogers.com.

I may not have the answers but I am a good listener.

My life may not have the greatest beginning, middle or end but I have learned that it is my wife and sons who have defined who I am and I'm so proud of them. I am honoured if they would be my legacy. My MS has beaten me down but they always bring me back up and give me a reason to smile and again I say "Life's been good to me so far." For this

I LOVE THEM WITH ALL I AM.

I AM THAT I AM

THE SPOUSES'S PERSPECTIVE

(MS Through My Wife's Eyes)

When Mark asked me to write a chapter for his book, I felt reluctant due to the fact that there are so many ups and downs dealing with this disease and MS is different for everybody. I am also a very private person and don't particularly want my family to be judged for anything that has been written or for anything to be misinterpreted. Nonetheless, I am confident that my perspective on my experience as a wife dealing with a husband with MS may in fact help another spouse or caregiver going through this, and for that reason, I feel that my story may be beneficial.

First I would like to share a bit about myself before discussing how MS has affected me and my family.

For starters I was born in 1970 in Malta. At that time, I had a sister who ended up turning one only nine days later. I was told that she didn't take kindly to having to share our Mother with her new baby sister. Two years later, our third sister came along, and apparently I had felt towards her much the same way my sister had felt about me when I arrived into the family. I guess my younger sister had stolen my spotlight, or so I thought. My parents moved us to Brampton, Ontario when I was eight years old. I remember feeling like we were on a different planet when we stepped foot into the Toronto airport. It was so different here from Malta.

It took me a few months to adapt, although we were kept quite busy being surrounded by various aunts, uncles and cousins. We were always a very close knit family. I distinctly remember my Mom, Dad and his siblings taking turns on a monthly basis hosting family functions and how much we used to enjoy going to them. We reached our teenage years and I truly don't know how my Dad got through it with three daughters so close in age. My Mom and Dad played a huge role turning me into the person I am today through their constant love, understanding, encouragement and support, although I do remember having quite the attitude as I got into my teenage years. I can recall many great memories with my family, particularly the trips we had taken to Malta and cottages we used to go to a few summers in a row with the aunts, uncles and cousins and having so much fun together. The worst memory I have is when my Uncle passed away in July of 1986 when I was sixteen. We were very close and whenever I was going through my troublesome times, he seemed to be the only one who could get through to me and make me feel better. That was definitely a devastating year for me. Then came January of 1987 when I celebrated my seventeenth birthday. Although I thought my world had crumbled having to deal with the loss of my uncle, that same month I was introduced to Mark. Little did I know that this would be the beginning of a new chapter in my life.

Mark and I instantly hit it off, and within ten days or so, he had officially asked me to be his girlfriend. We were inseparable and I remember loving every moment I spent with him. I remember he told me he loved me within two weeks of dating. Teenagers don't normally have a clue about true love, but I knew that this was the real deal. It didn't take me long to feel the same way about him. He was so good with me and instantly became very protective of me. Not one day went by that Mark and I didn't see each other. Because of all the time we spent together, we wound up losing a few friends along the way, but as the saying goes; friends come and go but family is forever.

A year passed from the day we were officially a couple and Mark asked me to marry him. I said yes immediately and was so happy that I would be spending the rest of my life with him. We took our time, and six years later in September of 1992 we became husband and wife. In February of the following year we made our big move to Malta. Things were going great and two and one half years later, I gave birth to our first son. Our years spent in Malta were wonderful and we created so many new memories, ones that I will never forget.

In February, 1998 we moved back to Brampton and soon after bought our first home. I gave birth to our second son a year later. We thought life was great, and although we dealt with the usual day to day stresses, we had each other and our two boys. Many happy moments followed.

Merely three years later, the nightmare began.

Mark was diagnosed with Multiple Sclerosis in October of 2002. We had absolutely no idea what we were up against. I had never even heard the words Multiple Sclerosis prior to that day and terrifying doesn't quite describe the way I felt . . . and not to mention . . . how Mark felt being given his diagnosis. I was in total shock. A million things had gone through my mind, but nothing seemed to make any sense. I distinctly remember the neurologist taking me aside and telling me some of the things of what I might expect, one of which would be Mark's possible mood swings, something to do with chemical imbalance. This may in fact be the reason why Mark had such anger issues throughout his life and still to this day. He may have had MS for many years, but just didn't know it.

Years followed, and needless to say, we went through a lot of ups, downs and hardships. By now, Mark was dealing with other health issues and taking various medications. Mark was becoming verbally aggressive at times and most of the time took his anger out on me. I was so frustrated because I was always supportive of him and was dealing with so much stress, plus trying to keep positive at the same time, yet he treated everyone else seemingly better than how he treated me. I can't even begin to tell you how angry it made me. Despite all this, our strength got us through it all. For most, giving up and walking away from it all would have seemed the practical choice, but for me that was certainly not an option. I knew he turned into who he became because of this "chemical imbalance" and I had to remain supportive, even though it was really difficult at times. Mark had always battled with anger issues even from when I first met him, but as his MS progressed, so did his anger. Regardless, I'm not one to give up very easily so at times I just dealt with it by lashing back at him. I'm sure it wasn't the best way to deal with it, but it sure did make me feel better. We always got over it and moved forward because no matter what we were going through, our love was deeper than any anger we were experiencing.

We did end up having something to look forward to, the birth of our third son. He wasn't exactly planned, but quickly turned into our little miracle. Our little bundle of joy helped bring our family that much closer together and gave us new strength. We were now blessed with three amazing boys and getting through everything for their sakes was an absolute must.

Mark has described the years to come very explicitly in his chapters, but where he was experiencing all the different emotions dealing with his disease, my hardships were trying to deal with our family life more or less on my own since Mark couldn't help the way he used to. I quickly became the breadwinner and watching Mark's health deteriorate was not easy by any means. I was now dealing with built in anger on top of everything else, and constantly asking myself . . . what will end up happening to the love of my life . . . what did we do to deserve this . . . how will we manage in years to come . . . what's in store for our kids' future. Then dealing with the horrific thoughts going through my head . . . am I going to lose my husband to this disease . . . why has MS taken so much away from us as a couple and as a family. These are the years we should be enjoying our life to the fullest, dancing close to each other the way we used to, going for walks together hand in hand, sleeping side by side, sitting together cuddling watching a movie, going to family functions together, preparing meals together, going shopping together, outings with the boys, maybe even doing a bit of travelling. These are all simple things so many take for granted. And we could no longer do any of them together. I knew that things weren't going to get any easier so I had no choice but to build up enough strength for the both of us. It worked for a while, but as Mark's disease kept progressing, I became more overwhelmed with the day-to-day challenges. I think to a certain point, I've battled depression too, but in a different way than what Mark's been going through. It doesn't help watching Mark being so angry and hating the world, talking about wanting to die and beating his legs when they're giving him hardship. I remember many times when I would have liked nothing more than to just stay in bed and not bother with life. But I kept telling myself that I simply had no choice. I must get on with it for Mark and our boys.

My advice to spouses and/or care givers supporting a sick loved one would be to first and foremost stick by that person no matter what . . . no matter how angry and nasty they may get at times. Just remember that it's their depression and chemical imbalance that's talking and not them. I've heard about many spouses who walk away from their loved one because they simply can't handle dealing with the added responsibilities any longer. You must remember that he/she didn't ask to get sick nor wanted to create these tribulations for their families. Try to be as strong as you can be for yourself and for that person for as long as you possibly can. That's not to say that you can't be human and go through your own down times, but try to do your best to remain strong and not to make yourself get sick. I've battled Thyroid Cancer, had surgery and managed to get through it all with major strength; but that's in my past. Tomorrow is my future . . . without cancer.

Gather as much research on Multiple Sclerosis as you possibly can for available medications and treatments. And do not believe everything you hear. Verify it for yourself. Get help from local organizations, find out about home care, deal with a pharmacist that you feel comfortable with and who understands your medical needs.

We have been getting home care for Mark for a while now. At first it was hard to accept because I felt guilty that I couldn't look after him the way I used to (he was also angry with me for it because he's mortified having others looking after him) and our seemingly revolving door with nurses coming in and out at different time frames (not an easy thing to get used to, but we get to know each of one of them and treat them like family). Be sure to have someone you can vent to who will listen to you no matter what and will not judge you or your loved one because of how you feel and the things you say (even if it is momentarily derogatory towards your loved one), because the way you feel today may not be the way you will feel tomorrow. Try to get support from family members, even if they can just take some time to keep your loved one company which will give you some time for yourself. You need it to re-energize.

All in all, I know Mark and I share a love like no other. We have been through so much over the years, but still remain strong and because of that, our love becomes stronger. Stress tends to bring out the worst in us at times, but we always get past it. I took my vows very seriously and I know that he did too and we've stuck by them no matter what. I must believe that I will remain strong and will do whatever it takes to cope with what's to come.

My advice to the person diagnosed with MS. Life isn't going to be easy, but always keep in mind that just as much as you didn't ask for this disease, neither did your family members. They will stick by you as long as you treat them well. You will definitely need their help and guidance, so be sure to be kind and loving to your family. You will have good days and bad days. And for better future mobility, be sure to keep your muscles moving as much as possible.

Most of all . . . . DON'T EVER GIVE UP. You are more important than you probably think you are. People love you.

A couple of quotes I have lived by and which speak volumes for me:

- Don't judge me, unless you have looked through my eyes, experienced what I have and cried the tears I have cried, felt the pain I have, felt the depression I have, and have felt the frustration and hopeless I have. Until then just BACK OFF because you have no idea how I feel.
- People usually listen better when you're dead.
- This is what MS looks like (MS)
- If I could walk a mile in your shoes, I would steal them and walk ten.
- Everyone better come to my funeral, to make sure that I stay dead.
- Together there is nothing we can't do
- Suck it up Nancy
- Plan for the worst and pray for the best
- Yesterday is history, tomorrow's a mystery. Live today like it is a gift as it is The Present. I ask, did I keep the receipt as I want a refund.
- There is a lot of pain behind this smile

A song has always reminded me of my life and what my wife means to me.

Here are the lyrics by the Verve Pipe: (lyrics from internet)

<u>COLORFUL</u>

The show is over, close the story book
There'll be no encore
And all the random hands that I have shook
Well they're reaching for the door
I watch their backs as they leave single file
But you stood stubborn, cheering all the while

I know I can be colorful
I know I can be gray
But I know this loser's living fortunate
Cause I know, you will love me either way

Most were being good for goodness sake
But you wouldn't pantomime
You are more beautiful when you awake
Than most are in a lifetime
Through the haze that is my memory well
You stayed for drama though you paid for a comedy
I know I can be colorful
I know I can be gray

But I know this loser's living fortunate
Cause I know, you will love me either way

Look ahead as far as you can see it
We'll live in drama but we'll die in a comedy and

I Know I can be colorful
I know I can be gray
And I know this losers living fortunate
Cause I know, you will love me
Yes I know, you will love me
I know, you will love me
Either way

Kind of sums up my life.

THE END

I know every book should have a happy ending, like a fairy tale but mine has a continuous struggle to fight together, to show strength like no one else can ever imagine and to stick together through thick and thin, so this is my positive ending, **MY FAMILY** and I'm good with that.

"Together there is nothing we can't do"
I hope you enjoyed my life story, my ups, downs, lefts, rights and your drink.

On to our next chapter of life, (stay tooned)
P.S. I love you Arlette, Randy, Jason, Dylan

Daddy is always here for you.
No matter what tomorrow brings . . . I'll be there for you.

- I laughed, I cried, I saw what true strength is.
- I give so much to others and through this book I gave so much to myself, Mark Stewart.
- One word prevails and that is "STRENGTH".
- An EPIC JOURNEY OF STRENGTH.

Author, Mark Stewart, is taking you on an emotional roller coaster of his life, the good, the bad, the happy, the sad . . . the entire nine yards of his life dealing with **Multiple Sclerosis.** This is an open invitational view into his life during his reflected search into what may have awakened the proverbial Monster Sleeping. It's a deeply personal inside look at a family's incredible battle to fight against this crippling disease and the unbelievable strength it takes to bring them closer together.

This book was sponsored by:

OMS (Ontario Medical Supply)
1100 Algoma Road
Ottawa, Ontario K1B 0A3
Direct Line: 613-244-8620
Fax: 1-800-373-4945